LE CORDON BLEU

Wine
ESSENTIALS

LE CORDON BLEU

PROFESSIONAL SECRETS

TO BUYING,

STORING, SERVING

AND DRINKING WINE

CARROLL & BROWN PUBLISHERS LIMITED

Contents

First published in the United Kingdom in 2001 by

CARROLL & BROWN PUBLISHERS
20 Lonsdale Road
Queen's Park
London NW6 6RD

Art Director Tracy Timson
Managing Editor Becky Alexander

Editor Dawn Henderson
Art Editor Evie Loizides
Designer Roland Codd

Photographers David Murray and Jules Selmes

Copyright © 2001 Carroll & Brown Publishers Limited

A CIP catalogue record for this book is available from the
British Library

ISBN 1–903258–13–8

Reproduced in Kuala Lumpur by Color Gallery

Printed by Artes Graficas, Toledo
D.L. TO: 334 - 2001

4

112 Serving wine

5

160 Fortified wine and grape spirits

6

174 The story of wine

Foreword

I am proud to present to you our latest venture: *Le Cordon Bleu Wine Essentials* – our first book to bring together expert advice from leading wine educators, critics, sommeliers and other wine professionals. It explains everything you need to know about how to buy, sell, store, taste and serve wine and – most importantly – enjoy wine. Whether you read this book from cover to cover or dip into it when occasion demands, you will be rewarded with easy-to-understand guidance that demystifies the techniques that often surround wine.

While there are many books on the market that tell you about grape varieties, vintages and styles of wine, very few tell you how to buy wine, and what to do with wine once you get it home. This book is the first comprehensive guide to all the essential know-how you need to handle wine with confidence. It explains how to build a collection; how to create the ideal storage conditions; how to open, decant and pour wine; how to taste wine and describe your findings; how to choose and care for glassware; and how to select and assess wine in a restaurant.

Le Cordon Bleu has wide experience of handling and serving wine, and it is this experience that we bring to *Le Cordon Bleu Wine Essentials*. Throughout this book you will find features on how to match wine with food, along with recipes from our Masterchefs for when you want to serve a special meal that befits a fine wine.

I hope *Le Cordon Bleu Wine Essentials* will give you the knowledge and expertise required to appreciate wine as a fascinating subject and, of course, as a versatile, complex and enjoyable drink.

A votre santé!

André J. Cointreau
President, Le Cordon Bleu International

7

There are many opportunities for buying and selling wine, wherever you are located. You can access good-quality and interesting wines via mail order, the internet, specialist importers and at auction, as well as many local shops that now offer an excellent choice for everyday drinking and for the modest collector. Furthermore, improved transport facilities and changes in government regulations mean that it is easier than ever to buy wine direct from wine-producing regions in Europe and elsewhere.

The 1980s saw a surge of interest in selling wine, and many wine enthusiasts (and entrepreneurs!) bought and sold wine at a profit. In recent years, investors have had their fingers burned, as the competition intensifies, but there are still many ways to make sensible investments. In this chapter, we guide you through the many buying opportunities; the basics you need to know when choosing wine; which wines to buy for immediate drinking, and which for collecting; and how to invest wisely.

Buying

and selling wine

FOR BUYERS

The identity of a wine is dependent on a few fundamentals: the type of grape from which it was made (the grape variety); the place where it was produced (the region); the company or person who made the wine (the producer) and the year in which the grapes were harvested (the vintage).

THE GRAPE

There are some 10 000 different types of wine grape, but only a very few of these – perhaps 50 – are commonly used by international wine producers. Much emphasis is placed on the variety of grape by wine lovers, and with good reason. The grapes are the principal ingredients of every wine, and the aroma, colour and flavour (in other words the character) of the wine are largely dependent on the type of grape or grapes from which it was made.

Usually, certain grape varieties are used to make red wines, and others are used to make white wines. The classic red varieties include pinot noir, cabernet sauvignon, shiraz (also known in some regions as syrah), merlot, zinfandel and gamay. Among the most popular white varieties are chardonnay, sauvignon blanc, riesling, semillon and pinot gris (or pinot grigio). Some grapes work best on their own; others are delicious when blended with others. For more on the different varieties, see pages 84–9.

One of the words you will often hear wine experts use is "varietal", which refers to a wine named after the dominant or sole grape variety used to make the wine. A Merlot, for example, is a varietal wine, as is the ubiquitous Chardonnay. The minimum percentage of the identified grape will vary from one region to another, but tends to range from 75 to 90 per cent. Most wines originating from regions in the so-called "New World" (that is, outside of Europe), such as California, Australia, South Africa, New Zealand and Chile, are marketed and sold as varietals. In contrast, much of Europe is regulated by an appellation system which specifies which varieties may be used. Bordeaux, for example, is rarely a "varietal" but a blend of two to four permitted varieties.

Region		Principal grape varieties
France	Bordeaux	Cabernet sauvignon, Merlot, Cabernet franc
	Burgundy	Pinot noir
	Loire	Cabernet franc
	Champagne	Pinot noir
	Rhône (north)	Syrah, Grenache
	Alsace	
Germany	Mosel	
	Rhine	
Italy	Piedmont	Barbera, Nebbiolo, Dolcetto
	Valpolicella	Corvina Veronese, Rondinella, Molinara and others
	Bardolino	Corvina Veronese, Rondinella, Molinara and others
	Soave	
	Emilia-Romagna	Lambrusco
	Chianti	Sangiovese, Canaiolo nero, Trebbiano
Spain	Rioja	Tempranillo, Graciano, Garnach tinta (Grenache)

THE REGION

In Europe (the "Old World"), by contrast, wines are generally known by the place where they were made rather than their grape variety. So, despite the fact that many European wines are made from the same grapes as those used in the New World, the bottles will read Burgundy or Rioja rather than Pinot Noir or Tempranillo. This practice isn't as irrational as it sounds, because wines take on the character of the place where they were grown. The soil, climate (frosts, sunshine, rainfall) and topography of a vineyard all affect the taste of the grapes – so much so that vines of the same variety can yield startlingly different wines even when the vineyards are directly next to each other.

Wine shops tend to organise their stock by country and region of origin, rather than by grape variety, but the place name on a label can usually tell you just as much, if not more, about a wine as the varietal name: it will guide you as to the grape varieties used, the style of the wine and the method of production.

Different vines are suited to different climatic conditions, so wine-producing areas have historically concentrated on growing certain grapes. This is now controlled by law in most European countries, so that place names denote particular grape varieties. All wine from Chablis in northwestern Burgundy in France, for example, is made with the chardonnay grape, although you won't find the grape named on the label. Unfortunately there are no hard and fast rules to help you memorise which grapes are used where – this knowledge simply comes with experience and the more you learn about wine. But the chart below left lists the principal grape varieties associated with some of the most famous areas in Europe.

As an added complication, regions can be further subdivided into districts, subdistricts, villages (or communes) and vineyards. So, for example, Burgundy has five districts (Chablis, Côte d'Or, Côte Chalonnaise, Mâcon, Beaujolais), several subdistricts, dozens of villages and hundreds of vineyards. Here's an example:

Region	Burgundy
District	Côte d'Or
Subdistrict	Côte de Nuits
Village	Gevrey-Chambertin
Vineyard	Chambertin

Broadly speaking, the more specific the place name on the label, the finer the wine is likely to be.

Champagne Taittinger, Hautvillers, France

Principal grape varieties

Semillon, Sauvignon blanc

Chardonnay, Pinot blanc

Chenin blanc, Muscadet, Sauvignon blanc

Chardonnay

Viognier

Riesling, Gewürztraminer, Pinot gris

Riesling

Riesling

White

Garganega, Trebbiano

Garganega, Trebbiano

Viura

THE PRODUCER

The name of the winery or château – the producer – is perhaps the most important piece of information on the label. It is far more important than the name of the region or the year of vintage because it is your greatest guarantee of quality. A good producer will make decent wine even in a poor year, whereas a poor producer could make disappointing wine even in a good year.

THE VINTAGE

The year in which the grapes for a wine are harvested is known as the vintage. Almost all wines carry a vintage date, but there are exceptions – non-vintage wines, such as most Champagnes, ports and other fortified wines, are blended from grapes harvested over two or more years in order to ensure consistency from one year to the next.

What does the vintage tell you?

The taste, texture, complexity and overall quality of a wine can vary from one year to the next, depending on the weather, when the grapes were harvested and so on. These variations are quite marked in wine regions that have an irregular climate, such as Burgundy and Bordeaux in France, Germany, Piedmont in northern Italy and New Zealand. In these areas, wine can range from "poor vintages", when the quality is generally disappointing, through to "great vintages", years in which outstanding wine was produced. In warm, sunny areas, however, such as southern Italy, California and most of Australia, South Africa and Spain, there is more consistency from year to year and thus vintage dates become less important as indicators of quality.

Nevertheless, even normally warm and stable regions can experience bad weather during the harvest season, and there are occasional bad vintages in hot regions.

Do vintage dates matter?

There seems little doubt that vineyard regions, especially in Europe, appear to be growing warmer. Scientists at Bordeaux University have charted the dates on which the flowering of the vine takes place each year, and have discovered that the flowering is occurring, on average, some ten days earlier than was the case only ten years ago. The significance of this is that if the vine flowers earlier, it ripens earlier, promising a precocious harvest; and the earlier the harvest, the higher the chances of being able to pick in fine weather. So although global warming isn't eliminating vintage variations, it does seem to be raising the overall quality level of most vintages.

Another factor that might be diminishing the importance of vintages is the use of mechanical harvesters. These allow grapes to be brought in much faster than in the past (particularly in bad weather), although such harvesters are frowned upon by many high-quality producers. Drying tunnels and so-called concentrators, which can remove the rain-water content from sodden grapes, have also made significant improvements to overall quality. Winemakers like to say that there is no longer such a thing as a bad vintage, and although that is an exaggeration, it is true that abysmal vintages (such as 1972 in Bordeaux) are probably a thing of the past.

Given that most of the wines for sale in your local wine shop will probably be available in one vintage only, is it worth hunting down a different vintage?

This depends largely on how much you are planning to spend. Fine wines from areas where the climate can change dramatically from one year to the next (mostly Europe) will vary in depth and personality according to the vintage, so the date should be a consideration. When choosing less expensive wines, however, the year needn't be an important factor in your decision as the differences between vintages won't be so significant.

Vintage charts (see below) can help you to choose between wines of different dates, but one point to bear in mind is that the criteria for defining "top" vintages (and hence "top" prices) can be personal, and may not match your own taste. What's more, when purchasing older wines, you can find bargains by choosing unfashionable vintages, such as 1981 Bordeaux, which was overshadowed by the resplendent 1982.

Vintage charts

Found in wine reference books and magazines, these offer a rating for a particular wine over a whole range of vintages. They can be extremely useful to refer to when choosing wine with which you are unfamiliar, but bear the following points in mind:

■ *They can give only snapshots of specific vintages. For example, 1996, which is thought to be a very fine vintage in Bordeaux as a region, was not nearly as good in the districts of St Emilion and Pomerol (on the right bank of the Gironde river) as it was in Médoc and Graves (on the left bank).*

■ *They are quantitative not qualitative. In Germany, for instance, 1989 and 1990 are both great vintages but have completely different characters – the 1989 being luscious but low in acidity, the 1990 being firmer, with higher acidity and greater potential for longevity.*

■ *They take no account of the influence and skill of the producer. So vintages such as 1987 in Burgundy, 1991 in Bordeaux, and 1998 in California may have been written off generally as mediocre, but you will often find that top properties still made excellent wines.*

Vintage declarations

Some wines that are not usually sold as products of specific vintages are occasionally released in costly vintage-dated versions. The most important are Champagne and port.

■ *In exceptional years, and only then, a small quantity of Champagne may be set aside for later release as a vintage wine. This will be more expensive and is usually intended to be cellared. Although not necessarily superior to a top blend, vintage Champagne should have the character of the specific year. Thus, vintages such as 1976, 1982 and 1989 are exceptionally rich and powerful, while years such as 1983, 1988 and 1993 will be leaner, more austere, and, in some cases, more intense.*

■ *Vintage port is produced only in outstanding years. Rich in sugar, tannin and alcohol, such wines are intended to be cellared, and can easily age for 20 years or more, developing more and more complexity the older they get. In some countries, however, such as the USA, many consumers like to drink them young so as to enjoy their primary fruit flavours. Although vintages are only "declared" in top years, sometimes port producers slip up – 1975, for example, proved to be a great disappointment.*

Vougeot, Burgundy, France

What does the
BOTTLE TELL YOU?

Provided you know what to look for, you can learn a huge amount about a wine simply by examining the outside of the bottle. The size, shape and colour of the bottle can give basic information about the region or grape variety, while the information on the label can help to fill in the specifics.

BOTTLE SIZE

In most countries, the basic wine bottle size is 75 cl (also labelled as 750 ml). Wine bottles have been used for centuries, but standardization of sizes is a relatively new phenomenon. When all bottles were hand-blown, size inevitably varied; with the advent of machine-made bottles, it became possible to reproduce exact sizes, but only in the 1970s did the European Union (EU) start to enforce standardization within its member countries. Non-member countries gradually fell into line for the sake of convenience. Many regions have their own traditional bottle sizes, though most are multiples of the standard bottle size.

Wine is available in bottles both smaller and larger than the usual 75 cl. Red Bordeaux and Champagne are bottled in several sizes, as seen below.

Bear in mind that wine keeps and matures much better in bigger bottles, because a smaller proportion of the wine comes into contact with the air in the bottle. A few half-bottles can be useful for those occasions when you want to drink only a glass or two, or for dessert wines such as Sauternes, which are so rich and sweet that a small bottle can serve a number of people.

With the exception of dessert wines, most half-bottles are best drunk within a few months of purchase. On the whole, it is much better to choose standard bottles or, if you can find them, magnums. Bottles larger than magnums may be good for celebrations, but can be unwieldy to handle and are often hard to find in shops. You will sometimes see magnums and jeroboams, but few producers make them regularly.

Bottle shape and colour

Most bottle shapes are dictated by the traditions of the classic European wine regions. Outside Europe, producers choose their own bottle shapes, and most select shapes that trigger the right associations. Red Bordeaux wine, for example, comes in bottles with square shoulders, so wines from other countries that use the same grape varieties grown in Bordeaux – Cabernet Sauvignon, Merlot and Cabernet Franc – usually have the same bottle shape.

The colour of the glass can also help you to identify the style of the wine. For example, red Bordeaux is always bottled in green glass, sweet white Bordeaux in clear glass and Rhine wines in brown glass.

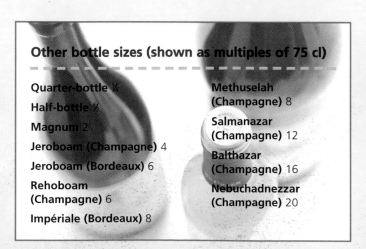

Other bottle sizes (shown as multiples of 75 cl)

Quarter-bottle ¼

Half-bottle ½

Magnum 2

Jeroboam (Champagne) 4

Jeroboam (Bordeaux) 6

Rehoboam (Champagne) 6

Impériale (Bordeaux) 8

Methuselah (Champagne) 8

Salmanazar (Champagne) 12

Balthazar (Champagne) 16

Nebuchadnezzar (Champagne) 20

Anatomy of a bottle

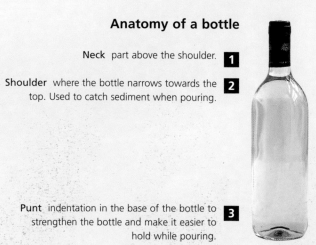

Neck part above the shoulder. **1**

Shoulder where the bottle narrows towards the top. Used to catch sediment when pouring. **2**

Punt indentation in the base of the bottle to strengthen the bottle and make it easier to hold while pouring. **3**

Recognising bottle shapes

Burgundy

Used for the red and white wines of Burgundy. It is also used across the world for white wines made from grapes grown in the Burgundy region, which are Pinot Noir and Chardonnay.

Bordeaux

This is the classic shape used for wine made from grapes grown in the Bordeaux area. Traditionally, these wines were intended for long ageing in the cellar, during which time a deposit would collect in the bottle. The square shoulders help to catch the deposit when pouring the wine, leaving any deposit behind in the bottle. This shape is also used for Bordeaux white wines.

German flute

German wines come in tall, narrow bottles, known as flutes. These are made from brown glass for wine from the Rhine valley, and green for wine from the Mosel, Saar, and Ruwer valleys. Some producers of Riesling wine in other countries also use this shape for their wine.

Flask

Traditionally used for wine from the German region of Franconia, and for Portuguese rosé wine. Few other producers use it, primarily because it does not fit easily on shop shelves.

Rosé

The original bottle shape for Provençal rosé wine, but rarely used today. Associated sometimes with holidays, serious producers of rosé now use other shapes.

Port

A heavy shape, using thick glass, designed for long ageing in the cellar. The square shoulders and the bulging neck help to catch sediment when being poured.

Champagne

This has thick glass to withstand the pressure inside the bottle, and a punt to strengthen the bottle. The corks are cylindrical prior to bottling, then they are pushed in under pressure and take on the familiar mushroom shape. The wire cage holds the cork in place.

DECODING A LABEL

Read the label properly and you'll know a great deal about a wine before you pour it. Don't be daunted by the amount of information – it's there to help you choose from the vast range of wine available.

Front and back labels

The front label must, by EU law, contain certain pieces of information:

- *The quality classification.*
- *Region of origin.*
- *Alcohol content.*
- *Year of vintage (if any).*
- *The name and address of the producer (or bottler).*
- *The size (capacity) of the bottle.*

In addition, it must have the name of the country of origin, and wine classified as "table wine" *must not* state the year of vintage. Legal requirements in non-EU countries may be different.

Many wine producers find that these requirements get in the way of attractive design, so they put this information on a functional label which is therefore, legally, the "front label". However, when the bottle is on the shelf, the label with the attractive design will face outwards – even though it is, by strictest definition, the back label.

You may also find other pieces of information on the label, such as a brief history of the winery, suggestions as to what food will best accompany the wine and advice on when to drink it. Use common sense to determine the difference between useful advice and marketing hype.

Alcohol levels

Many European regions impose minimum alcohol contents, but otherwise each region and grape variety produces wine with a different alcohol level. As a general guideline, the warmer the region, the higher the alcohol content. White wine from Germany may have an alcohol level as low as 7.5 per cent, whereas Californian Zinfandel could be as high as 16 per cent. Most table wine is between 12 and 13 per cent.

Reading a Label

▶ **Vintage Port**
A classic port design. The Taylor's crest is set into the thick glass.

▶ **Australian Semillon**
Margaret River is the region in Western Australia where this wine is made.

1 vintage   2 name of wine   3 classification   4 region of origin

▲ **Australian Cabernet Merlot**
As Cabernet is listed before Merlot, it means there is a higher proportion of Cabernet in the wine.

▲ **Red Bordeaux**
This is a very traditional red Bordeaux label.

▲ **Oregon Pinot Noir**
The mandatory government warning has been put on the back label.

▲ **White Burgundy Grand Cru**
Corton Charlemagne is the vineyard, and also the appellation.

▲ **White Burgundy Premier Cru**
Because this is a Premier Cru rather than a Grand Cru, it must attach the name of the village (Meursault) to the name of the vineyard (Blagny).

▲ **Champagne**
The year of vintage is on the neck label, but otherwise, this is a conventional front label.

5 name of producer **6** grape variety **7** where bottled **8** country of origin **9** bottle size **10** alcohol content **11** style of wine

Fortified wine is likely to be 20 per cent or more, although fino sherry is often 15 per cent. The alcohol content of table wine has been generally slightly higher in recent years, because of the fashion for full-bodied flavour. High alcohol content is not in itself a sign of quality.

Health warnings

Some bottle labels, particularly those from the USA must carry the warning "Contains Sulphites." Sulphur is added to wine at the winery as a disinfectant and anti-oxidant. In large quantities it can affect asthmatics but you have to place this in context – fruit juice, for example, contains far more sulphur than wine.

UNDERSTANDING WINE CLASSIFICATION

One of the most important pieces of information that you will find on a wine label refers to the legal classification of the wine.

European classification

Most European countries operate a four-tier system, modelled on the French Appellation d'Origine Contrôlée (AC) system that started in the 1930s as a protection against fraud. The idea behind this system is that the characteristics of the vineyard, as well as the grape variety, determine the flavour and style of the wine, so by giving it an appellation of origin – basically, a registered place name – consumers can be assured of the sort of wine they are buying.

Label design

Sauternes
The sweet, gold-coloured wine of this prestigious region in Bordeaux often has white labels with elaborate gold lettering.

Red Bordeaux
Traditional designs sometimes feature a photograph or illustration of the wine producer's château, often from original nineteenth-century engravings.

Riesling
German wine used to have labels using elaborate gothic script. Contemporary versions preserve the essential design – often containing a picture of the vineyard – but have made the lettering more readable.

New World
At the forefront of contemporary label design, New World wineries use elements from traditional label design alongside innovation, according to the market they wish to attract.

1 In the top tier are wines from a controlled region (or appellation). The use of this appellation is legally controlled, and stipulates:
- Which grape varieties may be grown.
- How big a crop may be taken.
- How the wine must be made and matured.

There are over 400 wines classified according to Appellation Contrôlée in France. Other countries in the EU use similar systems (see the chart below).

Italy and Spain have a tier of classification above their equivalent of AC. In Italy such wines are called Denominazione di Origine Controllata e Garantita (DOCG), and in Spain, Denominación di Origen Calificada (DOC). Parts of Germany are currently introducing a Grosses Gewächs (Grand Cru) and Erstes Gewächs (Premier Cru) system.

2 The next tier down in France is known as Vin Délimité de Qualité Supérièure (VDQS). Controls on grape varieties, yields and production methods are less strict than for the top tier. Many of these regions eventually become AC classified.

3 The next tier down is of country wines – Vins de Pays in France, Indicazione Geografiche Tipici (IGT) in Italy and Vino de la Tierra in Spain. Controls on these are more flexible.

4 The most basic wine classification is "table wine". In Europe these wines are not allowed to bear the name of a grape variety or a specific region, and are governed only by basic health guidelines. Available in restaurants and supermarkets in the country of origin, table wine is rarely exported.

	France	Italy	Spain	Germany	Portugal
1	AC (Appellation Contrôlée)	DOCG (Denominazione di Origine Controllata e Garantita)	DOC (Denominación de Origen Calificada)	QmP (Qualitätswein mit Prädikat)	DOC (Denominação de Origen Controlada)
2	VDQS (Vin Délimité de Qualité Supérieure)	DOC (Denominazione di Origine Controllata)	DO (Denominación de Origen)	QbA (Qualitätswein bestimmter Anbaugebiete)	IPR (Indição de Proveniencia Regulamentada)
3	Vin de pays	Vino da tavola and geographic name or IGT and name of approved area	Vino de la tierra	Landwein	Vinho Regional
4	Vin de table	Vino da tavola	Vino de mesa	Deutscher tafelwein	Vinho de mesa

Going higher

Some European countries have separate classifications over and above their appellation systems. Bordeaux in France, for example, is a region that produces so many wines that it supports several further classification systems. The Médoc district of Bordeaux produces many of the world's finest wines, which are labelled by château. The châteaux are ranked in descending order of superiority starting with first growth or "cru", then second growth and so on through to fifth growth (see chart below). The Graves district of Bordeaux also has its own classification, with one category of Cru Classé (or classed growth) for red wine and one for white wine. Still in Bordeaux, St Emilion classifies its best wines into Premier Grand Cru Classé, Grand Cru Classé and Grand Cru.

Burgundy, too, recognizes that some of its own vineyards deserve top rating. The very best are designated Grand Cru, and the second best are labelled Premier Cru.

The New World system

Other countries including the USA, South Africa, Australia, Argentina, Chile and New Zealand (collectively known as the New World) came to winegrowing without traditional rules and guidelines. Most have introduced appellation systems based loosely on the AC system, but leave the choice of grape variety and production techniques to the individual producers.

In the USA there is a system of AVAs (American Viticultural Areas). The name of an area appears on a label, but this guarantees only the origin of the grapes. The AVA indicates the likely style of the wine only insofar as a wine produced in a warm AVA will produce richer wine than one produced in a cooler AVA.

In Canada, producers who are members of the Vintners' Quality Alliance will put the initials VQA on their wine labels. The VQA impose higher quality standards than the national legal guidelines. Australia is gradually introducing a system of delimited regions, but the name of the region will not guarantee a particular style or quality.

Does classification help the consumer?

Appellation systems tell you quite a lot about the style of the wine, and if the wine has a classification on top of that, it ought to be better quality. But both systems help the producer, too – in France, when a region is promoted to AC, the price of the wine usually rises.

Other terms

Mis en bouteille au château/Estate-bottled This phrase indicates that the wine was bottled by the producer rather than a merchant.

Reserva/Riserva A term used in Italy, Spain and Portugal to denote that the wine has been aged for longer than non-Reserva wines before it is released for sale. For example, a Barolo Riserva from Italy will have received extended ageing in comparison with a straightforward Barolo. This isn't to be confused with Reserve on US wine labels. Reserve is used frequently by American winemakers because it implies prestige,

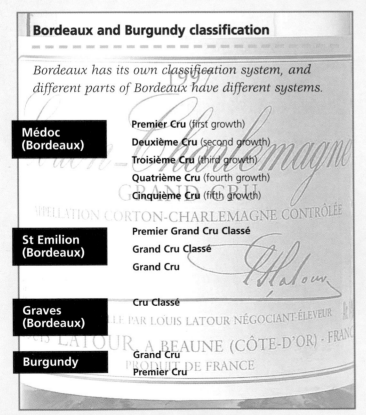

Bordeaux and Burgundy classification

Bordeaux has its own classification system, and different parts of Bordeaux have different systems.

Médoc (Bordeaux)
Premier Cru (first growth)
Deuxième Cru (second growth)
Troisième Cru (third growth)
Quatrième Cru (fourth growth)
Cinquième Cru (fifth growth)

St Emilion (Bordeaux)
Premier Grand Cru Classé
Grand Cru Classé
Grand Cru

Graves (Bordeaux)
Cru Classé

Burgundy
Grand Cru
Premier Cru

but the term isn't regulated in the USA and can be applied to any wine, rendering it unhelpful as an indicator of quality.

Superiore/Supérieur Wines with a higher minimum alcoholic strength than standard wines are often labelled superiore (in Italy) or supérieur (in France). Italian wines with this designation may have been aged for longer than normal, as well.

breaking the rules

In some circumstances a wine classification system can have a negative effect on quality. In Italy, in the 1970s and 80s, the appellation rules in certain regions, notably Chianti, insisted that producers add a percentage of white grapes to their red wine, and forbade them to use other grapes, including cabernet sauvignon. Many leading names decided to ignore the law, and made their wines the way they wanted.

The producers were not able to call their wines Chianti, and called them Vino da tavola, or table wine – the lowest classification of all. However, they gave the wines elaborate names and charged high prices for them, and they became the most fashionable wines in Italy, and other parts of the country copied. As a result, the law was changed. Many of these wines (for example, Tignanello or Solaia) are now labelled Indicazione Geografiche Tipici.

BUY WINE

Wine clubs, the internet, direct order companies and wine warehouses have greatly expanded the opportunities for buying wine over the past 20 years – but with so many options, how do you decide on the best place to spend your money?

NAVIGATING THE WINE SHOPS

If you are providing wine for a party, a wine warehouse that offers discounts on bulk orders should probably be your first port of call. When you are buying bottles in small quantities, a supermarket will have a good range. But if you are looking for mature wines or for scarce and highly esteemed wines, the best selections are at auction houses or fine wine specialists.

Independent wine merchants

For quality and service, these remain the best places to buy wine, although their numbers appear to be shrinking. Many of them are also importers and seek out wines of excellent quality and good value – some specialize in wines of particular countries. The staff tend to be well-trained and are good sources of advice. Most merchants publish regular wine lists, some of which are a mine of information. Prices, however, tend to be slightly higher than in a supermarket, and can vary greatly, so if you are in the market for a costly wine, such as 1961 Château Latour, it pays to shop around. Some fine wine specialists also have websites.

Supermarkets

These are good places to buy wines for everyday drinking. Competition between supermarkets has meant that prices are relatively low, but at the lower end of the market, quality can be questionable. Many buyers working for supermarkets are obliged to buy to a certain price to meet customers' expectations, even though in some cases good wines cannot be found at those prices from their suppliers. Expect minimal advice, and delivery is more the exception than the rule. Avoid supermarkets for very expensive wines, as prices are rarely competitive, and selection will be limited. Check bottles carefully before buying (see right), as some branches do not take storage seriously.

High street chains and warehouses

There is a wide range in quality between the chains, some of which are excellent, while others are more like outlets for beer and cigarettes with a few wines on the shelves. Because most warehouses buy in bulk, they tend to carry wines made in large quantities and of moderate quality. Most of them, fortunately, also try to cater to the customer looking for better-quality wines, and may have a fine wine corner or lists of fine wines that you can order but which are not routinely stocked. Some warehouses insist on your buying a minimum of a 12 bottle case, or at least offer a better discount on a case. Most of the chains and warehouses will deliver.

BUYING CONSIDERATIONS

A wine shop can be an excellent source of information, and staff are usually very happy to offer guidance. Look out for tastings, special offers and seasonal sales to get a good deal.

Bargain buys

Take advantage of seasonal sales. These usually take place after Christmas when specialist shops send out their bin-end lists of discounted wines or display them instore. There is usually nothing wrong with the wines – it's a way of clearing excess stock, or of disposing of a vintage shortly before the arrival of the new vintage of the same wine. Although sales sometimes contain wines that are in their dotage and should be avoided, there are also bargains to be found. Also, look out for special offers to promote a new vintage.

Tasting before you buy

Some shops organise free tastings on a regular basis. These can really help you to choose, but beware of wines left open for tasting for many days, as they may have become stale. Some shops and wine societies organise tastings of expensive or rare wines for regular customers or members. You may have to pay to attend, but they are a good way to learn about, for example, mature Burgundies or old vintage ports. If you are planning to collect serious wines, such tastings can be highly educational, directing you towards wines you like and deterring you from wines you don't, whatever their reputation or price.

Buyer beware

A good wine can easily be spoiled by poor storage, yet many wine shops still pay far too little attention to looking after their stock. When you are shopping for wine, note the conditions inside the shop to ensure that the wine you are buying is in its optimum state. Ideally, the shop should be climate controlled, but in reality only specialist shops tend to go to this expense. At the very least, the wine should be kept away from sources of heat and light (boilers, windows and so on).

None of the following indicators is a sure sign that the wine in the bottle is spoiled, but all of them should ring warning bells:

■ *Avoid bottles that are stored upright and are covered in dust. Wines should be stored on their sides, but for display purposes they are often kept upright. This will do no harm in the short term, but if a bottle gathers dust for months, the cork, deprived of contact with the wine, may dry out and the wine will oxidise (see page 45).*

■ *Reject bottles that are sticky, as this could mean that wine has seeped out. This can be an indication of damage caused by changes in temperature.*

■ *Do not choose wine with a protruding cork. This is usually a sign that the wine has been exposed to harmful changes in temperature, forcing the cork out of the bottle.*

■ *If, when you stand the bottle upright, the level of the wine is much lower than about 3 cm down the neck, evaporation or seepage may have occurred.*

■ *Avoid wine that is displayed directly under artificial lights, or in the sun, both of which can heat and damage the wine.*

Chiller cabinets

Most shops keep a small selection of wine (mostly white and sparkling) in refrigerated cabinets. Unless you intend to drink the wine as soon as you have left

the shop, it's a better idea to select bottles from the shelves and chill the wine at home yourself. This is because the wine in chiller cabinets may not be in the best condition – it is often too cold, and may have been stored upright in the cabinet for longer than is good for it. The vibrations generated by the refrigerator motor can also be damaging.

Returning a faulty bottle

If, after buying a wine, you discover on pulling the cork that it is undrinkable, you should return it as soon as possible. You may find that the wine is corked or oxidized (see pages 80–81). Unfortunately, pronouncing a wine faulty can be a subjective matter, and if the wine is just slightly off, you may find you have little recourse. But most merchants and retailers will, without too much argument, exchange or refund your money if you bring back a problematic bottle. If you discover the flaw only after you have poured the wine into your guests' glasses, be sure to pour the wine back into the bottle and replace the cork tightly. Returning a half-empty bottle and demanding your money back may be met with a sceptical response. All this applies to recently purchased wines. If you laid down the wine for some years and then found it to be corked, you would have to write it off as bad luck.

Returning faulty bottles that were acquired by mail order or from a website can be difficult once a bottle has been opened. You can avoid disappointment by choosing a reputable company that also has a clearly outlined policy on returns.

check the fine print

Look at wine lists or website conditions carefully to see what additional costs may be payable. Check whether the "case price" is for an unmixed or mixed case and whether there are additional taxes to be paid. Delivery charges can also vary greatly, and if you are asking a wine merchant to store your wine for you, check the rates and remember that they may not include insurance.

BUYING FROM HOME

There are several good reasons for making a purchase from the comfort of your home: delivery is usually included as part of the service, so you don't have to worry about lifting heavy cases of wine; it can enable you to get hold of wine that you can't find locally; it saves time; and it allows you to shop around for competitive prices.

Direct ordering

The easiest way to buy good wine is to phone or fax through an order to an independent wine merchant. Delivery is usually free, except for orders of minimal quantity or value. To make this facility more widely accessible, most specialist wine companies produce catalogues listing their stock; these are usually updated a few times a year.

Wine clubs

Many newspapers run clubs or special offers, often of pre-selected inexpensive wines at competitive rates. Few of them offer wines of exceptional quality, as the attractiveness of the offers is based on price. Some local retailers also operate clubs, which offer discounts, tastings and special offers to members. Tasting circles and local wine clubs may also track down interesting wines offered at attractive prices for their members.

The internet

There are many wine sites on the internet, some of which offer wines for sale. Choice varies, as does the amount of information about the wines on offer. If you find the wine you want at a good price, this is a perfectly sound way to buy.

BUYING FROM PRODUCERS

The most enjoyable way to buy wine is to go straight to the source. In a wine producer's tasting room you can sample wine at leisure and then choose which, if any, you wish to buy.

Buying direct

Europe has been far slower to develop the commercial possibilities of direct sales than the New World where the practice is highly developed, particularly in California. Much depends on the size of the winery – a small winery may have no facilities to sell directly to the public and may choose to sell by mail order and to dealers, but most medium or large wineries have well-equipped tasting rooms (see page 92).

Not all wineries, however, do allow you to buy the wines they produce. For example, in Burgundy, France or Piedmont, Italy, the best estates tend to sell out quickly to established customers; they may be happy to show you around, but they will not be able to sell you wine. In Bordeaux, most wine is sold to négoçiants (see pages 184–5) and cannot be bought directly from producers. So before making a trip to a winery or château, check that the wine is for sale.

The economic factor

In some areas, including California, wine is sold through a nationwide network of local distributors who do not want their prices undercut at the winery, so you won't find any bargain prices. You can, however, be sure that you will like the wine, and you may be able to buy wines produced in such small quantities that they are only sold at the tasting room.

In Europe, you will find that prices vary, but are usually cheaper direct from the producer than they would be from a wine shop in the same country. If you are visiting the Champagne region in France, however, you may well find that local supermarket prices are lower than those charged by the wineries.

Bringing your wine home

Before you get carried away and buy a year's supply of wine, you should consider how you will transport the wine back home:

■ *If you are travelling by car, keep your wine as cool and still as possible. Pack the wine in boxes (usually available for free from the vendor) and stack tightly. Avoid parking your car in direct sunlight for an extended period, as this can damage your wine.*

■ *Taking the channel tunnel to France is a good way to buy wine. There are no restrictions on the quantity of wine British residents can import from Europe, so as long as the wine is solely for personal consumption you can really stock up.*

■ *Shipping wine to different countries within Europe can be quite difficult and costly.*

■ *Sending wine – for example, from South Africa or California to the UK – is certainly possible, but can be fairly expensive. Think carefully whether the savings on the wine purchase justify the cost of transportation – a specialist wine merchant in your area might already stock the wine.*

■ *If you are travelling by plane, it is a simple matter to carry a few bottles, carefully wrapped, in your hand luggage, however, airlines are increasingly enforcing limits for hand luggage. It is extremely risky to put bottles in checked luggage, as they may break as a result of rough handling or changes in air pressure. Airlines will accept cases of wine as checked luggage, but it is your responsibility to pack the wine carefully and safely. Wine transported in this way will be considered as part of your weight allowance, so it is easy to incur excess baggage charges.*

BUYING EN PRIMEUR

A wine buyer can secure a bargain by purchasing wine before it has been bottled (en primeur, also known as futures), which involves paying for the wine at least one year before you receive it. It can be an excellent way to purchase wine, but it is not without its risks.

Why buy en primeur?

The theory is that by paying for wine upfront, before it is bottled, you obtain the wine at the best possible price. This method of buying wine only became common over the last 20 years, and it is now a routine way to acquire wines that are in short supply.

It makes sense to buy en primeur, however, only if you are sure that either or both of the following conditions will be fulfilled:

■ *The wine is so scarce that unless you purchase at the first opportunity, you will be unlikely to secure it at all. Some of the world's top châteaux and wineries, for example, produce so few cases (3000 or less) a year that the wine sells out long before it can hit the shops.*

■ *The price will be much cheaper than if you wait until the wine is released on the market. It is difficult to predict whether a wine bought en primeur will prove less expensive in the long run, but many wine enthusiasts take the risk.*

Be informed

It is important to gather as much information as you can before placing an order en primeur. In the early summer following the vintage (harvest), wine merchants will release their en primeur offers. Compare and contrast offers from different merchants. Bear in mind that whatever they and wine journalists write about the new vintage, their views will be based on tastings made when the wine was very young. Buy only from a reputable merchant – even if cheaper offers are available from unknown sources. The same caution applies to buying en primeur on the internet.

Market values vary, and if a wine has proved disappointing, this will affect the value of other wines from that producer in the preceding and following years as merchants adjust their stock levels. This is part of the gamble.

How to purchase en primeur

- *Once you have decided to buy a case from a new vintage, you need to contact your chosen wine merchant and pay the sum cited in the offer.*
- *The merchant should then send you a certificate that asserts that you are the owner of this case of wine.*
- *About 15 months later, you will be notified that the wine has arrived and will receive a further invoice for any duty, tax and delivery charges.*

BUYING AT AUCTION

Wine lovers have bought at auction for centuries and it can be an excellent way to build up a collection. Many auction houses organise pre-sale tastings for catalogue holders, where you can sample some of the wines.

It is important to bear in mind why wines are being sent to auction, however. In some circumstances a restaurant, wine merchant or private collector may want to unload surplus stock, or the contents of a substantial cellar may be sold by executors; in these instances you are likely to encounter some interesting wines at good prices. Occasionally, however, wines are sold because the previous owner dislikes them or has found them faulty. Be wary of 11-bottle lots – one bottle has clearly been tried and found wanting.

Buying wine at auction can be risky. You should ask about the provenance (ownership and storage history) of the wine, but you'll find that wine is often poorly documented. Fine wine specialists can usually give you more detailed information.

auctioneer advice

- **Look out for mixed lots of assorted wines. Some of the wines may be of little interest, but others may be highly desirable or unusual. As long as the price is right, this can be an enjoyable, if slightly chancy, way to buy older wines.**

- **Pay attention to neck and shoulder levels specified in the catalogue – a low level of wine suggests seepage or evaporation which can affect quality.**
- **You can bid either in person or by fax, although being there in person gives you greater flexibility.**

- **Check merchants' catalogues before deciding on your bid – over-excited buyers often pay more at auction than they would pay at specialist shops.**
- **Most auction houses use symbols to indicate additional payments on top of a successful bid. Check the fine print.**

Starting a
WINE COLLECTION

To ensure a steady supply of the wine you want, when you want it, you need to establish a collection. Many wines benefit from some ageing, and the most cost-effective way to acquire a mature wine is to buy it when released and relatively inexpensive, and store it until it is ready to drink.

THE OCCASIONAL COLLECTOR

The majority of wine drinkers buy their wine shortly before consuming it. This is a perfectly sensible thing to do, but its limitation is that you are at the mercy of your local retailers and their range of wine, which in some rural areas or remoter suburbs can be restricted. Better to accumulate a small and diverse cellar, so that you will have wine on hand whatever the occasion.

You should choose your wines according to your personal taste, of course, but bear in mind that a varied collection will enable you to respond to every whim and mood – both your own and those of your guests or friends. You may particularly enjoy Australian Shiraz, for example, but there will be occasions when you may need to offer a different style or colour of wine to a guest who doesn't share your enthusiasms, or when you need to take a bottle as a gift, or open a bottle of Champagne to celebrate some good news.

THE SERIOUS COLLECTOR

If you like to drink mature wine on a regular basis, it may be more cost-effective to collect wine seriously. The size of your collection will of course depend on how much you tend to drink, the amount of space you can allocate to storage, and how much you can afford to spend. But whether you have a collection of 50 or 5000 wines, you will need to strike a balance between wines that are ready to drink straight away, and those that are still maturing. Here are some tips to get you started:

■ Buy your favourite wines en primeur (if prices are attractive) or as soon as possible after release to obtain the best price (see page 26).

■ Check the wine lists from the best independent merchants, as they regularly launch new wines and release new vintages.

■ Consult magazines and websites devoted to wine for tips on outstanding releases.

■ Just like investing on the stock market, diversity is the key to success. Wines can be temperamental, and you will minimise the risk of disappointment if you buy a range. Concentrate on a favourite region or wine by all means, but try not to do so exclusively.

■ If you are interested in buying a particularly expensive wine, or a dealer sells the wine in cases only, you can reduce the cost by splitting a case with a friend who shares your interest.

■ Try to stagger your purchases so that your cellar will always contain wines that are ready to drink as well as bottles that need to be aged for many years.

■ Avoid purchasing more wine than you can possibly drink, unless you are buying partly as a form of investment – there are too many sad tales of wine that was kept too long and only uncorked when long past its best (see pages 58–9).

■ Consider buying through a "cellar plan", which is offered by some of the larger wine merchants (see below).

Good candidates for collecting

You should buy the wines you enjoy, but bear in mind that some wines are not intended to be kept for long periods (see pages 30–31). The following wines are good candidates for collecting, as they will become more enjoyable with ageing:

■ *Red wines from regions in France such as Bordeaux, Burgundy, and the Rhône Valley. Most reds made from grape varieties such as cabernet sauvignon, syrah (or shiraz), sangiovese (Chianti, Brunello) and nebbiolo (Barolo).*

■ *White Burgundy, Graves and Riesling from Germany, and Alsace.*

■ *Fortified wines can be kept safely for some years, but only certain styles, such as vintage port and Madeira, will improve with age. Others, such as oloroso sherry and Marsala, will simply remain the same.*

For more detailed advice on wines for laying down, see pages 32–5.

Storage

If you are planning to buy many bottles for laying down, storage conditions are crucial (see pages 44–5). If you do not have suitable storage in your own home, you can either buy your wines from a merchant who can store them on your behalf, or you can rent cellar space. Urban cellar space is often more expensive than elsewhere in the country, but may be more convenient for you. Such facilities offer ideal temperature and humidity (see pages 42–3).

cellar plans

Some winelovers are keen to build up a cellar but are unsure about which wines to buy. Moreover, they may not have the time or inclination to scour wine lists and deliberate over potential purchases. In such cases, it may be sensible to consider joining a "cellar plan" – a scheme offered by a number of good wine merchants. These are packages of five or more pre-selected cases, fashioned to your budget. Often, storage is thrown in free for a few years and advice is given on when to drink the wines. The drawback is that you have less freedom of choice than if you select your own wines. On the other hand, such plans offer reasonably good value and the advice given is invariably sound and reliable.

BUYING WINE FOR EARLY DRINKING

Almost all of the wine that we buy and drink is intended to be drunk young. A staggering proportion of wine is consumed within 24 hours of purchase. Because of the vast choice available and the fluctuations in both price and quality, it is often more difficult to buy good wines for early drinking than it is to buy more serious wines for laying down.

What is considered "young" varies according to personal taste but, in general, the term means between 6 and 12 months after bottling.

You don't necessarily have to go to specialist wine shops when looking for bottles that you intend to drink quite soon. Large wine shops, accustomed to holding stocks for many months or years, may not be the best places to buy a lively young Beaujolais Villages or a

Drinking it young

Red wines

Pinot Noir
The grand reds of Burgundy should be aged, but most New World examples, whether from California, New Zealand or Chile, should be drunk young, when the aromas and flavours are at their most overtly fruity.

Merlot
Less tannic than Cabernet Sauvignon, Merlot's fleshiness and bright fruit make it an ideal candidate for early drinking. There are serious Merlots from Pomerol and California, but bottles from Italy, Switzerland and southern France are all intended for early drinking.

Gamay
For all practical purposes, Gamay means Beaujolais. The French call it gouleyant, meaning thirst-quenching, and few young reds can match Beaujolais for easygoing charm.

Cabernet Franc
The mainstay of red Loire wine in France, this is usually a lean, zesty, occasionally herbaceous wine, which makes an ideal summer red. There are more serious examples which can age well, but inexpensive wines from Chinon, Bourgeuil, or Saumur-Champigny (all in the Loire) are to be enjoyed young.

Rosé wines

Rosé
There are a small number of serious rosé wines, such as Bandol, which can benefit from ageing, but in general, rosé, whether made from syrah, grenache, cinsault or any other grape variety, should be drunk as young as possible.

crisp Provençal rosé. Supermarkets and warehouses are likely to have a speedier turnover and as a consequence the wines will be fresher.

The other thing to remember when selecting wines for drinking young is to buy in line with your needs – estimate how much of a wine you are likely to drink before the next vintage before buying large quantities. A rosé or simple Sauvignon will start to lose much of its appeal within a year or so of the vintage. Remember that there are also some expensive wines that generally do not improve with age. These include most Viogniers, many Chardonnays and red wines such as Dolcetto from Piedmont.

The following lists suggest the grape varieties or wine styles best suited for early drinking:

White wines

Chardonnay
Look for the simpler styles, such as unoaked wines from northern Italy, southern France and Australia, not to mention generic Chablis.

Pinot Blanc
This cousin of Chardonnay has low acidity and is almost always at its best within two years of the vintage. Alsace has the best examples, but in southern Germany and Austria the grape, known there as weissburgunder, is taken more seriously and is often aged for longer.

Sauvignon Blanc
With its vigorous acidity and piquant aromas, Sauvignon is an acquired taste. But it can be delicious and one of the most refreshing of all white wines. The best examples come from New Zealand and the Loire (Sancerre and Pouilly-Fumé), but much inexpensive white Bordeaux is mostly made from sauvignon blanc, too.

Riesling
Unrivalled in its capacity to age, but that shouldn't prevent you from enjoying it young. With its fresh acidity and zest, it is a perfect summer lunch wine. The top estate wines from Alsace, Germany and Austria are intended to be aged, but most generic German and Alsace Rieslings are best enjoyed young.

Müller-Thurgau
With its light acidity and delicate fragrance, Müller-Thurgau delivers a wine of no pretensions but with simple, appealing fruit. Many cheaper German wines are predominantly made from this variety.

Viognier
Very perfumed and rich (and often expensive), Viognier does not usually age well. Enjoy this sumptuous wine young, and look out for less expensive versions from southern France and Australia, which are improving in quality.

Sylvaner
A simple earthy white, regarded as a workhorse grape in Alsace, but more highly esteemed in Germany. Although some examples from Franken in Germany can age well, it is nearly always drunk young and fresh. It can, however, be difficult to get hold of.

Vinho Verde
Not a grape variety but a style of wine produced in northern Portugal. Like Riesling it is high in acidity and low in alcohol, but it is invariably a wine to be drunk young and cold. Many exported versions are slightly sweet, but the bone-dry versions are far more refreshing.

RED WINES FOR LAYING DOWN

When fine reds are allowed to mature in the bottle, several remarkable changes take place that make the wines even more pleasurable to drink:

- The colour will slowly change from a purple to a brick red. If you slightly tip a glass of aged wine and look at the colour of the edge of the wine, you will see how much browner it is than that of a young wine.
- The aroma develops in complexity. The fruity smell the wine had when it was young gradually reduces, while other more subtle aromas come to the front.
- The taste of the wine becomes less harsh as the tannins diminish.
- The overall texture of the wine gradually becomes softer and smoother.

- The wine develops more "length" (that is, the taste lingers for longer after you swallow it).
- More sediment is likely to collect in the bottle.

There is a catch, however. Age a red wine for too long and it will start to lose the delicate balance it has acquired and deteriorate in quality. Eventually it will turn into vinegar.

Reds worth ageing

The chart below suggests some fine reds that will benefit from a few years in your cellar. But it's not just expensive red wines that can develop in bottle and are good candidates for laying down. There are other wines with a tannic structure that require many years to soften, largely because of the grape varieties used in

The reds to lay down

France

Bordeaux Choose the classified growths of the Médoc and Graves and the best-known properties from St Emilion and Pomerol. A Bordeaux from a good vintage (there is no point laying down wine from a mediocre vintage) should be kept about 8 years and can continue to improve for a further 10–15. If the wine comes in a wooden case, leave the case unopened – this enhances the wine's value if you need to sell it.

Burgundy Much Burgundy can be drunk with pleasure about 5 years after the vintage. Only Premier and Grand Crus need longer ageing. In general, wines from Nuits-St-Georges and Gevrey-Chambertin require the longest ageing, while wines from Beaune or Chambolle-Musigny can be enjoyed relatively young. Great Burgundy can improve in bottle for 20 or 30 years; some vintages (1988) demand a further decade in bottle, while others (1989) are perfect now.

Rhône Three appellations from northern Rhône – Hermitage, Côte Rôtie and Cornas – are worth laying down. Hermitage is a powerfully structured wine that needs 10 years to show at its best. Côte Rôtie needs slightly less time. Cornas is the most rustic and its tannins can be harsh when young. From southern Rhône, Châteauneuf-du-Pape from a great vintage (1990, 1998) benefits from being kept for about 10 years, after which it becomes more gamy and complex.

Spain

Ribera del Duero and Priorat These produce Spain's biggest red wines, and they can improve with age. However, many renowned Spanish wines, such as Vega Sicilia, are aged extensively in barrel and bottle before being released, so even top Spanish wines are enjoyable young, although they can be kept safely for a further 5 years or more.

the wine. From France, look for wines from Bandol, Madiran and the best bottles from the Languedoc. From Italy, consider Barbera d'Asti and from Spain, Rioja. Australian Shiraz can age superbly, too. None of these wines need cost a great deal, yet they will develop more complexity with 5–10 years in your cellar.

How long should you keep it?

Predicting the perfect moment to drink a wine is one of the most exciting challenges of owning a collection. There are various factors that will affect the rate at which a wine matures. A great deal depends on the style and approach of the winemaker. The storage conditions (particularly temperature) in which the wine is cellared are also important, as is the size of the bottle. Generalisations about ageing potential can be difficult to make, but the chart below offers guidelines as to how long to cellar the recommended wines. (Pages 58–9 also contain details on judging when a wine is ready to drink.) It's important to remember, though, that winemaking has changed radically over the last decade. In the past, most Bordeaux was undrinkable for a decade or two, which is why it had to be cellared. Today, even the best wines from Bordeaux and Burgundy are made in such a way that they are approachable much younger – this is due to gentler vinification that extracts less harsh tannins. This doesn't mean that these wines won't age and even improve, but it does mean that cellaring for long periods is now less necessary.

Italy

Barolo and Barbaresco From Piedmont, these wines can have immense tannins as well as high acidity. Both these features will be tamed with age, and wines from a top vintage (1990, 1996) should be laid down for between 5 and 10 years. Brunello di Montalcino is Tuscany's mightiest red and should be cellared for about the same period; this is equally true of the so-called Super-Tuscans, such as Sassicaia and Tignanello.

United States

Cabernet Sauvignon Wine from the top Napa Valley wineries will develop well for a good 10 years (although it is also delicious when young) and in exceptional vintages can keep for up to 20 years.

Australia

Shiraz South Australian Shiraz, such as from the Barossa valley, is a prime candidate for laying down, although its rich primary fruit means it can also be drunk young. The most sought-after wines include Penfolds Grange and Henschke's Hill of Grace.

Portugal

Vintage port Only if it is vintage does port need to be laid down – usually for about 15 years, although some vintages will easily last for 30 or more. There is a growing tendency, especially in the USA, to drink vintage ports quite young (at between 5 and 10 years), but this is a matter of personal preference.

The whites to lay down

Bordeaux Most white Bordeaux is intended to be drunk young. The exception is the Pessac-Léognan region, in effect the northern Graves. White Bordeaux from top estates is undergoing a revival, and the very best deserve to be cellared. These rich, dense, oaky whites, from properties such as Haut-Brion and Domaine de Chevalier, are usually best at 10–15 years old.

Burgundy Mature white Burgundy can be a splendid wine, but not all whites from the region age well. Wines from villages with a relatively modest reputation – Auxey-Duresses, Rully, Pernand-Vergelesses – can be delicious but only the very best will still be gaining in complexity after 5 years. In general, it is the Grands Crus (such as Montrachet, Chevalier-Montrachet, Corton-Charlemagne) and the Premier Crus from Chassagne-Montrachet, Puligny-Montrachet and Meursault that will age well. Chablis, too, ages very well because of its high acidity. Vintage is an important factor. Low acidity years such as 1992 or 1998 are probably best drunk at around 5–8 years old; more structured years such as 1990 or 1996 will improve for 10 years or more.

Alsace Gewürztraminer and Riesling from the leading producers (such as Hugel) will mature well for 4 or 5, and sometimes up to 10, years. Grand Crus will age for even longer.

WHITE WINES FOR LAYING DOWN

It is often thought that white wine in general should be drunk young and cannot match red wines for longevity. That is probably true of the majority of white wines, but there are a fair number that can age magnificently, and in a few cases will keep for even longer than the great majority of reds. Good storage is the key to successful ageing when it comes to white wines, as white wines are usually more sensitive than reds to adverse storage conditions.

Whites worth ageing

Really outstanding white wine is far more rare than its red equivalent, so prices tend to be high. There are few relatively inexpensive white wines worth cellaring, but you should consider Hunter Valley Semillon from Australia, Riesling Kabinett from top German estates (for about 10 years) and Premier Cru Chablis. Among sweet wines, look for Loire wines from the chenin blanc grape (Côteaux du Layon, Vouvray, Bonnezeaux); many are seriously undervalued and can age with distinction for 20 years or more.

Sweet wines

Sugar is a great preservative of wine, and most sweet wines can be kept for 10–20 years without losing their fruit. But retaining fruit is not a sufficient reason to cellar a wine; you want the wine to evolve in an interesting and rewarding way. Riesling and the rare Beerenauslese and Trockenbeerenauslese from years such as 1921 and 1949 are still going strong. Equivalent wines from Austria, being a touch lower in acidity, may prove less long-lived but can be cellared easily for 15 years, though they are very enjoyable young:

■ *Sauternes is the classic sweet wine for ageing. Relatively high in alcohol as well as sugar, these lush, honeyed wines*

| Italy | **Pinot Grigio** Particularly those from Collio and Colli Orientali in Friuli can be aged for a few years, but it's time to drink up by 5 or 6 years. |
| **Germany** | **German Riesling** This has low alcohol, but high levels of acidity and extract, and sometimes sweetness. All of these contribute to the wine's longevity. Young Riesling is invigorating, fruity and racy; mature Riesling (at 10–15 years old) is more honeyed and petrolly. The very sweet styles such as Beerenauslese can easily be kept 20 or 30 years. |

| United States | **Top Californian Chardonnay** Can mature for up to 10 years, but most are best drunk younger. |
| **Australia** | **Hunter Valley Semillon** A uniquely Australian classic, this is a dull wine when young, but after about 8 years it becomes wonderfully rich and succulent. This is one of the few Australian whites that benefits from being laid down. Dry Rieslings can also be kept, but only for about 5–12 years. |

can develop beautifully in bottle for 20 years or more. Many vintages of the 1920s from estates such as Climens and Coutet are still surprisingly fresh. The wines are not fashionable, and can be bought for reasonable prices, given that the yields are four times lower than those for red Bordeaux. A fine old Sauternes can be a magnificent climax to a good meal. Lighter vintages such as 1987 or 1994 can be drunk with pleasure after about 5 years, but top vintages such as 1988 or 1990 are still not at their peak.

■ *Tokaj wines from eastern Hungary have legendary longevity. The top bottlings – 5 or 6 puttonyos (puttonyos being the official category specifying intensity of acidity, sugar and extract, with 6 puttonyos being the most intense) and Aszú Essencia, made from the best grapes of the best vintage, can be drunk young with pleasure but become more complex with age. They are more or less indestructible, as is vintage Madeira, the most long-lived of all fortified wines. The top wines can be kept easily for about 30–40 years.*

ROSÉ WINES FOR LAYING DOWN

Almost without exception, rosés should be drunk very young, but a handful can age well. Some rosés from Bandol in Provence can benefit from ageing, and the rare rosés from the Champagne region such as Rosé des Riceys usually improve after 5 years in bottle.

CHAMPAGNE FOR LAYING DOWN

Top quality vintage rosé Champagne will often improve over 5 to 10 years and regular vintage Champagne can keep for even longer. But many Champagne drinkers prefer even vintage wines relatively young; an aged Champagne may lose much of its freshness and vivacity. It's a matter of personal taste.

WINES

Certain wines increase dramatically in value as they grow older and rarer, meaning they have the potential to yield very significant financial returns. Wine frequently appreciates faster than real estate, and can outperform the stock market – but fine wine investment is not without its risks.

THE BEST WINES TO BUY

Despite the plethora of quality wines available today, only a tiny percentage of the world's wines actually make sound investments. Guidelines as to which wines are suitable for investment are given in the chart opposite. French wines, particularly red Bordeaux, from the best estates and vintages have historically dominated the investment market, and continue to do so today. White Bordeaux are not generally good investment wines, even though they are more scarce than their red counterparts, because they do not age particularly well. As a general rule, Burgundy doesn't offer quite the same returns as Bordeaux, but there are a few wines worth collecting (see opposite). The market for non-French fine wines has developed much more recently and is, therefore, less predictable, but some good bets are listed opposite.

When possible, look for wines in large formats, such as magnums or jeroboams, both because they slow down the evolution of the wine and thus increase its longevity, and because collectors particularly like such formats for their rarity and visual splendour.

Minimising the risks

Buying wine for investment rather than for pleasure is a gamble. Wine markets, just like any others, go down as well as up in value. Huge demand for wines from certain markets, such as Southeast Asia, has pushed prices up enormously in the last decade or two. But demand can slump swiftly in the wake of economic recessions or plummeting exchange rates. There is no way to guarantee success when it comes to wine investment, but there are a few things to bear in mind:

■ *You need to learn about the potential of a wine for maturing. In general, investment wines should be capable of aging for 20 years or more, so that you can wait and sell when the market is right.*

■ *Make sure that the conditions in which you store your wine are the best they can be, so that your wine will not spoil.*
■ *It is difficult to predict trends in the wine market, but it is important to gain a knowledge of market conditions, so that you are in the best position to make a profit. Wines given very high scores by leading wine writers, especially in the USA, may, as a result of a sudden increase in demand, become sound investments.*

Beware of forgeries

Many people involved in the wine trade – auctioneers, merchants and private collectors – worry about the not infrequent appearance of wine forgeries, especially at auction. Suspicions are aroused when substantial quantities of rare "trophy" wines keep appearing at auction. It is technically feasible to obtain old bottles and fraudulently re-label and re-cork them as famous wines. It is in the interests of producers and auction houses to prevent such wines coming onto the market, and greater vigilance is being shown. As a potential purchaser it is essential to check the provenance (ownership and storage history) of a rare wine.

The self-financing cellar

Wine lovers with a taste for fine wines and a pocket that is deep enough to finance it often buy a wine in part for investment, in part for future enjoyment. Thus, instead of buying a single case of a new vintage of a favourite wine, they will buy two, with the view of drinking one, and, at a judiciously chosen moment, selling the other at a profit. With luck, the sale of the second will even cover the cost of buying both cases. And if the wine fails to appreciate in value or fails to find a buyer, then at least it can be drunk with pleasure. This is a more sensible way to invest in wine than buying with the primary purpose of making a profit on a liquid asset.

The blue chip wines

Red Bordeaux These are the most sought-after wines, which may seem surprising given the relatively large quantities in which these wines are produced – Châteaux Latour and Cheval Blanc may be great wines, but they are not rare. Nonetheless, certain wines, such as 1900 Château Margaux, 1947 Château Cheval Blanc, and 1982 Le Pin, have acquired legendary status and are eagerly snapped up by collectors. Other Châteaux to look out for are Pétrus, Lafite-Rothschild, Mouton-Rothschild, Haut-Brion, Lafleur and Ausone.

White Bordeaux A few châteaux are worth collecting, notably Haut-Brion, Laville-Haut-Brion and Domaine de Chevalier. As regards Sauternes, some vintages of Château d'Yquem have appreciated in value, but these are the exception rather than the rule.

Burgundy Look for the top estates, such as Domaine de la Romanée-Conti and Domaine Leroy.

Champagne If Champagne is of good quality, it develops a rich biscuity flavour as it gets older – rather like old white Burgundy. This is much appreciated by the British, although the French themselves and most other Champagne lovers prefer to drink vintage Champagne relatively young. So, although there is a market for fine old Champagne, it is rather a limited one.

Port As a wine that has always been cellared for decades, older vintages of vintage port are frequently offered for sale and the best of them are fetching very good prices. At the beginning of the 1990s, however, the vintage port market was slow, and it was only in the late 1990s that it picked up again. Taylor, Quinta do Noval, Fonseca and Graham are the top names to look for.

German The ultra-sweet Beerenauslese and Trockenbeerenauslese ought to be sound investments, given that they are produced only in top vintages and in tiny quantities. Although greatly prized within Germany itself, however, there is a limited international market for the wines. The finest are sold at auctions within Germany, so they enter the market at a high price and the chances of substantial appreciation are uncertain.

Other European A few fetch high prices – Sassicaia from Tuscany and Vega Sicilia from Spain are especially prized.

American So-called "California cult" wines are produced in such small quantities that they are highly sought after and, therefore, command high prices. These include Caymus Special Selection, Dominus, Colgin and Screaming Eagle.

Australian Rare wines such as Penfolds Grange and Henschke's Hill of Grace usually sell extremely well.

Selling WINE

Most of us buy wine to drink, whether in the short or long term, but from time to time it may be necessary to sell wine. Although it is never difficult to sell wine that is greatly sought after, it is not so easy to dispose of wines for everyday drinking.

SELLING FINE WINE

Excellent wine from excellent vintages is always in demand. Fashions may change, but the blue chip wines (see page 37) will always find a buyer. Remember that the closer the wines are to their original packaging, the greater their value. Thus, if the wine was delivered in an original wooden case it will be worth more if sold in the same condition. Larger bottle sizes, such as magnums or jeroboams, are also likely to fetch a premium at sale.

When you decide that you would like to sell, shop around for the right price. Do not be tempted to accept the first quotation you are given – contact as many fine wine specialists as you can. By checking current auction prices for your wines, you can gain a shrewd idea of what your wine is really worth. Magazines such as *Decanter* and *Wine Spectator* follow the auction scene closely, as do a number of excellent websites (see pages 186–7).

If the wine you want to sell is very rare or special, the more information that you can give about provenance (the history of the bottles, how you acquired them, where they were stored), the better. Occasionally, wine forgeries turn up on the wine market (see page 36), and anyone who is interested in buying very valuable wine will find this sort of information reassuring.

Sales options

Before you make a sale, consider the alternatives. It could mean the difference between making a small profit and gaining a small fortune:

- *A simple way to sell fine wines is through advertisements in magazines such as Wine Spectator, where specialists in fine wines are always signalling their eagerness to buy your wines. Bear in mind that the value you place on the wine, probably based on what you consider its replacement value to be, will be higher than what you are likely to be offered. The fine wine broker needs to make a profit.*

- *If you propose to sell your wines to a fine wine specialist or broker but are unhappy with the prices, consider arranging for your broker to sell them "on consignment". This means you and the broker agree on a price, which is likely to be slightly higher than the cash price initially proposed, but you will receive no payment until the wine is actually sold. If the broker goes along with this, you must accept that you may not be paid for some weeks or months (which may be inconvenient if you are settling an estate or otherwise need to*

raise the money reasonably fast), and that some of the wine may be unsold. On the other hand you will, in the long run, receive a larger sum for the wine sold than if you had accepted the broker's initial offer outright.

■ *Auctions might seem to be the most straightforward way to dispose of your wines, but you need to be aware of the costs involved. You must bear the cost of packing and shipping the wine to the auction house, and insuring the wine during its journey. Any lots that remain unsold will be returned to you, and again you must pay for the transportation. Your commission to the auction house on each lot sold will be 10–15 per cent, and there may be taxes as well. In addition, there will be a "premium" on top of the hammer price. All this can add up to a hefty sum.*

■ *The internet has always been used by companies to sell wines to potential customers, but soon it will be a two-way process, and it will be possible to sell or trade wines from your own cellar via the internet. Some sites allow individuals to trade their wines, as well as offering other facilities such as storage. Such sites are currently in their infancy, but no doubt will proliferate in the future.*

Selling inexpensive wine

If you have a large mixed assortment of wines bought inexpensively over the years from the supermarket, you will find them almost impossible to sell. They are unlikely to have been cellared in ideal conditions, and many of them may be past their best. The majority of inexpensive wines are intended to be drunk soon after purchase, and will tire rapidly after two or three years in the bottle, so the market for such wines is all but nonexistent. Probably the best thing to do is throw a party for your friends and neighbours.

transporting wine for sale

At some point, the wine you are selling must be transported to the cellars of the auction house or broker. If your wine is potentially valuable and the quantity is reasonably large (40 cases or more), the auction house or broker will send someone to check the wine's condition and inventory your collection. If you agree to do business with that company, they may pack and remove the wine on the spot, in the case of, for example, a small quantity of exceedingly valuable wine. Otherwise, they will recommend professional shippers who will collect and deliver the wine. The cost will depend on the quantity of wine to be transported and the distance covered.

Shipping wine for sale across international borders is likely to be very costly and to involve a good deal of paperwork. If you live close to the cellars used by the auction house or broker, you can save a lot of money by delivering your wine – making sure each case is clearly labelled – directly and in person.

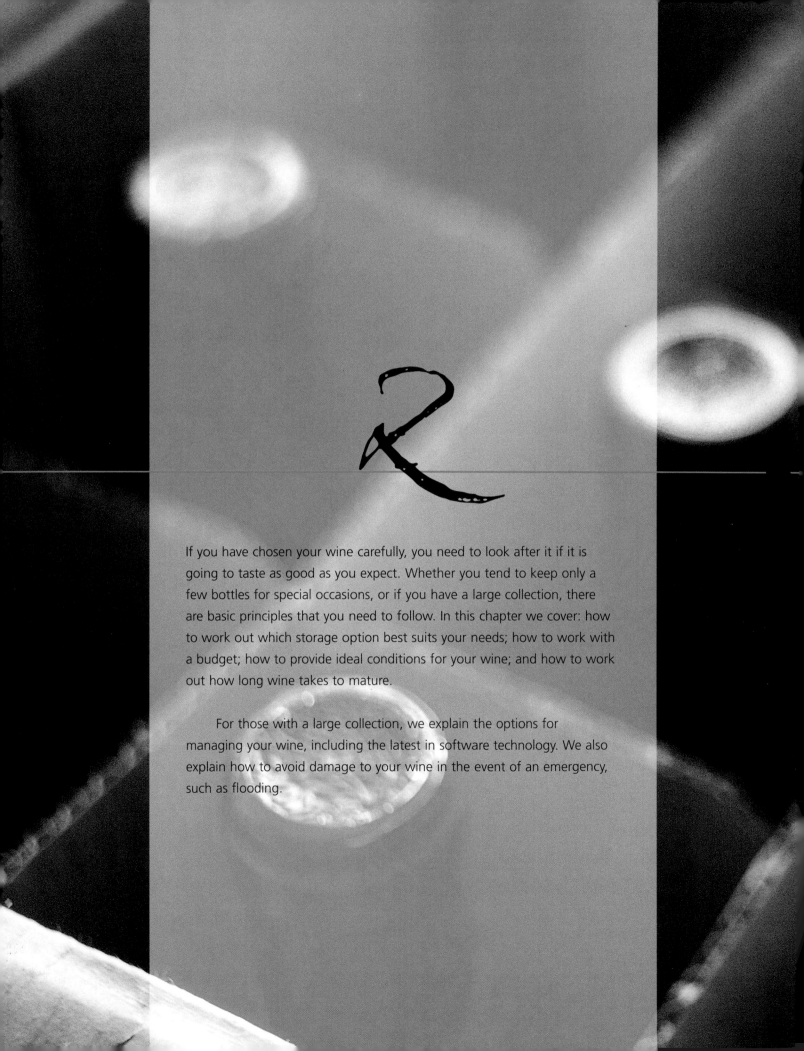

R

If you have chosen your wine carefully, you need to look after it if it is going to taste as good as you expect. Whether you tend to keep only a few bottles for special occasions, or if you have a large collection, there are basic principles that you need to follow. In this chapter we cover: how to work out which storage option best suits your needs; how to work with a budget; how to provide ideal conditions for your wine; and how to work out how long wine takes to mature.

For those with a large collection, we explain the options for managing your wine, including the latest in software technology. We also explain how to avoid damage to your wine in the event of an emergency, such as flooding.

Storm

wine

Looking After
YOUR WINE

Whether you tend to keep only a few bottles of wine for everyday drinking, or are a keen collector, you need to consider how best to care for your wine. Thoughtful planning will ensure that your wines fulfil their potential and are not damaged as a result of poor storage conditions; it will also help you to keep your budget in check.

ASSESSING YOUR NEEDS

First, you need to calculate how many bottles you will want to store over the next few years. If you mostly buy wine for drinking within a few days or weeks, you may need only a basic wine rack, but it may be worth thinking about how many times you buy wine to give as a gift. Would it make sense to bulk–buy wine for long-term use? If you have a collection of wine that you intend to keep for longer than 2–3 weeks, you need to think about the space you need to store it correctly (see below) so you can be sure it will be in good condition when opened. Ask yourself the following questions:

■ How much space do I need? (See below.)
■ How long will I need to store wine before drinking it?
■ Do I have enough space for my collection at home?
■ Can I provide good storage conditions for my wine? (See pages 44–5.)

■ How much money do I want to spend on creating the ideal conditions?
■ How often do I want to access my wine?

Keeping your wine at home

If there is a part of your home that you rarely use, consider whether it could be converted into a cellar. A small room, a cupboard or even just a corner of a room could be ideal. Using part of a garage or utility area is another option, but you will need to insulate it against severe cold, or in the winter your wine might freeze. There are various places to avoid:

■ *In or close to the kitchen. Temperature and humidity variations are particularly severe in a kitchen.*
■ *Near a stove, oven, boiler, hot-water pipe, washing machine, dryer, refrigerator, or anything else that generates heat or causes vibrations.*

Calculating your space requirements

If planning a cellar, calculate how much racking you will need by estimating how much wine you will buy in the coming months and years. Remember to include wine for gifts or special occasions. Here is an example of a year's consumption:

■ **Hosting a dinner party**	Once a month x 5 bottles = 60 bottles per year
■ **Gifts**	Twice a month x 1 bottle = 24 bottles per year
■ **Dining at home**	3 times per week x 1 bottle (48 weeks at home) = 144 per year
■ **Total consumption**	228 bottles (19 cases of 12 bottles)

GETTING WINE HOME *When you get your wine home, transfer it to a suitable environment as soon as possible to keep it as cool as possible.*

Third-party storage

A more cost-effective solution may be to store your wine at a specialist storage facility such as a wine merchant, a wine club, or a wine storage warehouse. That way you can be sure that your wine is in the hands of professionals. Consider the following, however, before making your choice:

■ *Visit the facility before you commit to make sure that everything is well organised. Verify the temperature, the humidity and the light. If the warehouse is near a railway or road, check that the vibrations are not too severe.*

■ *Ask how much notice you must give to release some or all of your wine collection. There may be restrictions on when you can pick up your wine. Some companies will deliver the wine to your door when you need it. Investigate delivery charges and whether you will have to pay a fee every time you withdraw wine.*

■ *Make sure that the warehouse looks secure. Windows should be barred, doors should be locked and an alarm system should be in place. Ensure, too, that all the wine cases are clearly marked with the owners' names.*

■ *Be fully briefed on insurance conditions. If the company was to go bankrupt, there would need to be detailed records of your personal cellar.*

■ *Check the annual cost per case – there may be a minimum charge. Some companies provide you with your own "cage" or "mini-cellar", which you can fill as you like. If your wine merchant has offered free warehousing, ask for how long it is free and what the charges will be thereafter.*

■ *In the attic or loft. The space directly below the roof can be very hot in summer and cold in winter.*

■ *Any room or cupboard with under-floor heating.*

■ *A room that receives a good deal of sunlight. Light and heat will work together to affect your wine adversely.*

Working with your budget

Whether your home has an appropriate basement or you just have a spare corner, you will need to budget for the work required to improve the wine storage conditions. The cost depends mainly on the quantity of wine you wish to store and whether you want to do the work yourself or pay a specialist company or building contractor. Ready-made cellar solutions such as a wine-storage cabinet tend to be at a greater cost per bottle. Higher costs are also associated with better design, so if it is important for the cellar to blend in with the décor of your home, you may need to budget extra (see pages 48–9). If you do not have space inside, there are specialist companies that can help you to build a cellar in your garden or under your property(see page 49), but this is often expensive.

cellarmaster tips

■ **If space at home is a problem, divide your wine collection. You could keep wine that needs ageing for a few years in a warehouse, wine for special occasions in a hard-to-reach, converted cupboard, and wine for everyday drinking in an easily accessible wine-storage cabinet.**

■ **Try to avoid the temptation to fill every space in your wine racks immediately – the result is a permanently full cellar and no room for impulse-buys.**

■ **If you have wine that you don't particularly like and it is taking up valuable space in your cellar, sell it, give it away or throw a party.**

Ideal Conditions for Wine

If you decide to keep your wine at home, you need to think about providing the best environment for it. This is important if you want to keep a few bottles for everyday drinking, and essential if keeping wine for long-term ageing.

WHY STORAGE MATTERS

How you keep your wine affects how it develops in the bottle, both in terms of how soon the wine becomes ready to drink and how the wine's components (acidity, tannin and fruit) develop and integrate.

Usually, the more expensive the wine, the more care you need to devote to ensuring correct storage conditions. This becomes even more pressing if you

buy wines for investment, intending to sell part or all of your collection at a later date. Storage conditions will also affect how the outside of the bottle looks, which is important for re-sale, and for looking good on your dining table.

If you have underground storage, you may already have ideal conditions in which to store your wine. If all of the following conditions are present, you have what is known as a "passive" cellar – you don't need to do anything to it. Otherwise, you will need to make changes (see page 50) to achieve the ideal conditions.

Conditions checklist

Temperature A constant temperature is the most important storage factor for wine. The ideal is between 10°C (50°F) and 15°C (59°F). Slow, seasonal fluctuations do not matter, but extremes of temperature and sudden changes cause harm (see opposite). Heat rises, so in any given space, the top will be warmer than the bottom. Whatever your storage conditions are, arrange your wine with whites and rosés at the bottom and reds at the top.

Humidity The ideal humidity for wine storage is between 60 and 80 per cent. If humidity levels go above this, you will not harm the wine inside the bottle, but the labels may be damaged by mould. If the humidity level is too low, the cork may dry out and shrink and the wine may evaporate.

Light It is best to store wine in a dark place. Bright sunlight can go through glass, especially clear glass, and can ruin the wine inside the bottle. If your cellar room has a window that lets in light, cover it with a curtain or blind to block it out, year-round.

Ventilation Allowing a small amount of air to circulate in the wine storage area keeps it free from stale smells, which can affect the flavour of the wine. Add an air vent to your room if necessary. Strong smells will also affect your wine, so keep it away from paint, chemicals, strong-smelling food and anything else odiferous.

RESTING IN PEACE *Wine should be stored in a dark, humid and cool environment to mature effectively. Store bottles horizontally so the cork doesn't dry out.*

Stability Keep your wines where they will not be disturbed by movement and vibration. If you live near a railway or busy road, keep wine off the floor and away from the walls to minimize the effects. Avoid storing near a washing machine or refrigerator.

Position If you intend to store wine for more than a few days, lay the bottles in a horizontal position. This keeps the cork in contact with the wine, so that it remains moist, which prevents oxidation. If the cork is allowed to dry out it will begin to shrivel, opening up a space between it and the sides of the bottle. Air can then seep in from the outside under the capsule (the wine bottle capsule is not an effective seal), and your wine will be ruined. When you are ready to serve the wine, turn the bottle back to an upright position to allow any sediment to settle on the bottom.

INCREASING HUMIDITY   If you live in a dry area, you could spread some sand on the floor of your cellar and sprinkle it with water to increase humidity levels.

Storage temperature guidelines

| DANGER! Risk of Freezing below -1°C (30°F) | Slow Maturation -1°C (30°F)–9.5°C (49°F) | Ideal Temperature 10°C (50°F)–15°C (59°F) | Fast Maturation 15.5°C (60°F)–22°C (72°F) | DANGER! Risk of Evaporation over 22°C (72°F) |

-1°C (30°F)   **22°C (72°F)**

cellarmaster tips

- The lower the temperature, the longer your wine will take to mature. If a wine is said to be at its best 10 years from the vintage date, this assumes storage at the ideal temperature. The wine will mature faster in warmer conditions and vice versa.
- If your wine is individually wrapped in tissue paper, remove it before you place the bottle in wine racks or bins. In high humidity areas, the tissue paper will stick to the label and ruin its appearance.

Cellar equipment

Wine carrying basket Useful to carry your wine from your storage area to where it will be served. Not to be used for storage.

Thermometer To monitor the temperature of your storage area. If your room is large, then use two or three thermometers placed around the room.

Hygrometer To monitor the humidity levels in your storage area.

Torch Enables you to examine the labels without disturbing bottles in the racks.

Stepladder The easiest and most stable way to reach the top racks.

MATCHING

Wine and Food

Red wines with red meats and white wines with white meats – a simple approach, but no longer adequate to reflect the wealth of ingredients and cooking styles now used widely. To get the most out of food and wine, you need to weigh up all of the complexities of both to find a beautifully balanced match.

MATCHMAKING

When it comes to food, the basic role of wine is to quench the thirst and cleanse the palate after each mouthful. But this is wine and food matching at its most basic. To appreciate fully the flavour and texture of fine wine and food, choose a combination that will bring out the best in your food, and enhance the subtleties of your wine.

Which comes first?

So which do you choose first – the wine or the food? The answer is that it depends on the situation. If you are in a restaurant, the best thing to do is to look at the menu and first decide what you are eating and then consult the wine list to pick out a bottle that will complement your meal. If, however, you are dining at home, or in a restaurant with a reputation for its fine wine cellar, choosing a dish to suit the wine would be the best option.

FLAVOUR

The principal flavours in your meal should be reflected in your wine, but not rigidly so. Rich meat flavours do work well with luxuriant, complex red wines, such as Bordeaux, but they can also sit beautifully with lighter reds, such as a fruity Burgundy, or an oaked white Chardonnay on a summer evening. If serving a wine with citrus-fruit aromas, add a little citrus juice to the food, for example, a squeeze of lemon, to enhance the flavour of the wine.

If you are choosing your wine to match your food, you need to think about the cooking processes and how these will affect your wine choice. Chicken marinaded and barbecued with a spicy sauce will require a softer,

LIGHT AND WHITE Grilled salmon, or salmon wrapped in filo pastry, suits a light, crisp white wine such as Riesling – a good match in terms of flavour, texture and weight.

RICH AND RED For a special red wine, with full body, high tannin and good flavour, serve a rich, red-meat dish such as roast duck or a grilled steak. The richness and juiciness of the meat enhance the texture and flavour of the wine.

fruitier wine than will roast chicken, which can handle a wine with more personality. You must also consider the other ingredients that go into the meal.

ACIDITY

Meals that have a sharp flavour, such as duck à l'orange or salads with a vinegar dressing, need to be paired with wines of similar acidity. Low-acid wines will be overpowered by such foods and will be left tasting dull and flavourless. Alternatively, serve an acidic wine with a smooth, creamy dish for contrast, and vice versa. Pasta served with a rich tomato sauce will call for a less acidic wine than pasta served with a cream sauce.

TEXTURE

The sensual nature of fine food is enhanced by a wine with a matching, or contrasting, texture. Silky, smooth Sauternes-style or other dessert wines have a creamy, luscious mouthfeel, so a dish such as crème brûlée would be compatible. An aromatic Gewürztraminer, with low acidity, would offer an interesting contrast.

A meaty textured fish such as shark or tuna would be best matched with a light red wine, rather than a white wine – the texture of the fish would overwhelm most white wines.

WEIGHT

Young, delicate white wines should be served with light foods that allow the flavour and texture of the wine to shine. A young, crisp Riesling or Chardonnay will lift simply cooked lobster or grilled chicken.

Full-bodied wines, on the other hand, must be served with big, robust-flavoured foods – a young red Rhône will be an excellent match for a rich venison ragoût, while a refined Bordeaux might be overwhelmed by the big flavours and richness of the stew. Not everyone enjoys full-bodied wine, so do feel free to serve the type of wine that you enjoy, rather than following these guidelines slavishly.

cooking with wine

Wine is often used in cooking to impart flavour to a recipe. The flavour of red wine is absorbed into the ingredients during the cooking process, and the alcohol evaporates, leaving a soft, palatable wine flavour imbued in the dish. If you are serving a wine sauce, or making a wine-based casserole such as coq au vin, use the same wine (or a cheaper wine of the same type) during the cooking as you will be serving with the dish. The flavours of your meal will then be in perfect harmony.

To make a dish more compatible with a special wine, add a little of the wine to the cooking juices just before serving. A dash of Sancerre in the pan after cooking monkfish will lift the cooking sediments and, with a little butter, makes a simple, but effective sauce to spoon over the fish. Fortified wines such as Port are delicious splashed into a recipe at the end of the cooking process – you will need only a small amount to add flavour.

For a subtle hint of flavour, you can reduce wine to use as a garnish. Reduced red wine is delicious painted onto a poached pear to create a magical flavour combination.

Racks and Ready-Made Cellars

Unless you have the space and the inclination to accumulate large stocks of wine, you can rely on ready-made storage solutions, such as racks. Small, ready-made cellars can be bought; they are dear compared to racks but do ensure that your wine is kept in ideal conditions, so you can be confident it will be safe.

WINE RACKS

If you are starting with a modest collection of wines or just want to store wine for everyday drinking, a simple rack will be adequate. If your wine will be on show, you should choose one to suit your personal taste and décor. Racks come in metal and plastic and all kinds of wood – some will sit on surfaces and others can be fixed to a wall. It is important to choose a wood that will not become easily mildewed – redwood is a particularly good choice. Avoid novelty wine racks as these generally offer poor value for money.

The traditional wine rack is made of wood, usually pine, and steel, divided into pigeon holes in which the bottles sit. Many companies make customised wine racks; the cost normally is determined by the number of holes. Such racks are generally of a much higher quality than kits and are flexible, with corner units and racks to suit different bottle sizes.

There is also a large range of alternatives to racks in the form of bins or hives, which allow you to stack between 8 and 24 bottles in each. Honeycomb or diamond shapes are common and can be combined to fit your storage area. There are various hives on the market, made of concrete or similar material, which help to maintain a constant temperature. When choosing a wine rack, bin or hive, consider the following:

- Is it sturdy and stable?
- Will it hold large or unusually shaped bottles?
- Will it hold half-bottles?
- Will it suit your décor?
- Does it fit the available space?

WINE STORAGE CABINETS

For the slightly larger collection, you may want to consider investing in a wine storage cabinet or "cave". These are self-contained, temperature- and humidity-controlled units that you plug into an electricity socket. The cabinets vary in size from a small domestic

RACK THEM UP *Store your bottles label-upwards so that you can minimize disturbance when selecting your wine, and avoid scuffing the label.*

cellarmaster tips

- If you have a dozen bottles or more of one wine that you will be drinking regularly over a fairly long period of time, consider buying a double-depth wine rack. You can keep some bottles behind to bring forward once you have drunk those in front.

- There is increasing evidence that Champagne and sparkling wine may be stored upright with no harm – in fact they might even benefit from it. However, they need to be in the same temperature-controlled environment as any other wine.

- All fortified wine can be stored upright except for vintage port. Traditionally, vintage port is marked with a strip of white chalk to indicate which side should be facing upwards; this is to minimize any disturbance to the sediment.

CABINET STORAGE Wine cabinets are temperature-controlled storage alternatives to cellars that enable you to store your wine in ideal conditions, and access it easily.

the DIY cellar

If you have bought a few bottles of fine wine to keep, but you have very limited funds to devote to storage, you can still take steps to look after your wine correctly.

■ Find a small, dark corner or cupboard somewhere in your home where you are confident that the temperature can be kept constant. It should not be in the kitchen because of smells, temperature changes and humidity.

■ If required, place a damp sponge in your chosen corner to create some humidity and re-wet frequently.

■ Use surplus building materials to build a sturdy wine rack. Choose materials with good insulating properties, such as old ceramic roof tiles (make sure that they have not become mildewed), bricks or plastic pipes.

OFF THE PEG The Spiral Cellar is a ready-made concrete cellar with a waterproof liner, which is inserted into a pit dug underneath your home. Because it is underground, it relies on natural conditions to provide the right temperature and humidity – aided by its concrete structure.

refrigerator to a small room, though the most popular are just above head height, and are able to store about 200 bottles. The most expensive ones have separate compartments that allow you to keep red and white wine at serving temperature. When choosing a wine cabinet, consider the following:

■ Check that your floor can stand the weight of the cabinet. When full, the average 200-bottle size cabinet weighs around 385 kg (865 lb).

■ If you are going to keep your cabinet in a living area, make sure that the noise level is not too intrusive.

■ Will it suit your décor? They come in a range of styles, many designed to look like a piece of furniture. You could choose to paint the cabinet yourself to suit your decor.

Designing a Cellar

If you have space to dedicate a room or large cupboard to housing your wine collection, you have an excellent opportunity to create an ideal cellar environment. Here we explain how you can adapt an existing area. Even if you decide to use a specialist company to design and build a cellar for you, understanding the basic concepts will help you get the cellar you want.

GETTING STARTED

Before you start shopping for shelving and racks, you need to assess the suitability of the area you plan to use. Start by measuring the existing conditions in your chosen location:

■ Take readings of the temperature and humidity in different weather conditions (a hot, sunny day and a cool, damp day), and at different times of the year.

■ Think about how you can light the area when you need to read labels or retrieve wine. Bear in mind that the wine should be in darkness for most of the time. Do you need an electric light, or will a torch suffice?

■ Check that the area is well-ventilated. Air should be able to enter and circulate, but there should be no draughts.

■ Finally, calculate the area. Measure the floor space, wall height and width both before and after you add insulation and vapour barriers (see below). Note the position of air vents, doors and windows.

Creating the right conditions

Prevention is always better than cure. By controlling the ambient conditions, you will minimize the risk of damage to your wine collection.

■ *To reduce and control temperature fluctuations, insulate your area with a material such as foam boards – available from large DIY outlets. Do not cover any existing air vents.*

■ *Unless your cellar is passive (has consistent ideal conditions, year-round), install a conditioning unit designed for wine cellars. Choose carefully, as some domestic air-conditioning units will de-humidify the air, causing a whole new set of problems. If required, choose one that supplies heat as well, so you can warm the area in the winter. If you are planning to*

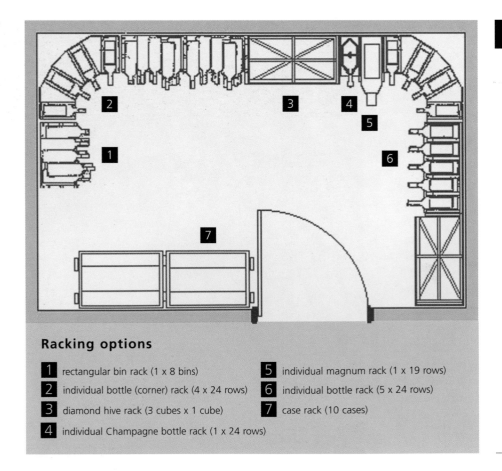

Racking options

1 rectangular bin rack (1 x 8 bins)

2 individual bottle (corner) rack (4 x 24 rows)

3 diamond hive rack (3 cubes x 1 cube)

4 individual Champagne bottle rack (1 x 24 rows)

5 individual magnum rack (1 x 19 rows)

6 individual bottle rack (5 x 24 rows)

7 case rack (10 cases)

cellarmaster tips

■ **When choosing a suitable room, check if the outer wall faces the sun. If this is the case, place your wine away from the wall, and add extra insulation to the affected wall to minimize the amount of heat that comes through.**

■ **Install an electric light on an automatic timer system, so that there is no danger of leaving the light on.**

■ **Remember to allow shelf or racking space for different bottle sizes. You can buy racks and bins specially designed for large and small bottles.**

STORAGE BINS Ideal for stacking several bottles of the same wine allowing less space to be taken up than placing them in individual pigeon holes.

Your storage options

The design of your cellar needs to take into account how you want to store your wine. If you buy fine wine, there is some value in keeping it unopened in its original wooden case – particularly if you intend to sell the wine. Don't be tempted to stack boxes on the floor where they might be affected by cold, damp or vibration. Instead, build or buy a suitable shelving system, remembering to take weight into account – a case of 12 bottles weighs at least 16 kg (36 lb).

For a large collection, use specialist racks, bottle bins and hives that can take up to 24 bottles each and can be added to as you accumulate more wine. Go for open units that allow the circulation of air in the cellar, which helps to maintain a stable temperature.

There are many designs of racks that can fit into even the smallest space. Corner racks, single bottle racks, case racks and unusual-shaped bottle racks are available from specialist suppliers to maximize storage space (see opposite). Some companies offer a cellar-design service. If designing your own cellar, be sure to allow room for you to manoeuvre in the space. If you decide to leave extra space, perhaps with a view to adding to your collection in the future, think about how you can minimize disturbance to the wine in the event of a rearrangement.

DREAM CELLAR Specialist companies can design and build both practical and attractive cellars to house even the most extensive wine collection.

place the unit in or near to your living area, check that it doesn't make too much noise.

■ *To prevent the rot and mildew that often result from high humidity, you may also need to install vapour barriers. If your humidity is too low, try the traditional wine producer's technique of spreading sand or gravel on the floor and keep it damp by sprinkling water over it.*

■ *If your chosen area is too light, block any windows with well-fitting blinds made with black-out fabric, or brick over the window. In this case, take the opportunity to install an air vent, if the room needs it.*

■ *Install adequate security systems. This is a requirement of most wine insurance policies (see page 57).*

CANAPÉS

The role of canapés is to kick-start the appetite in preparation for your meal, and the wines you serve should complement this aim. Choose clean, light wines to go with a varied selection of canapés, or fortified wines to enhance rich *amuse-gueules* such as foie gras.

Mixed canapés

If serving a range of flavours and textures, it is sufficient to offer just one type of wine, such as a full-bodied white. Champagne or a good dry sparkling wine are very refreshing with lightly salted canapés and always add a sense of occasion to a gathering.

Champagne or sparkling wine *Pick dry (Brut), with a fresh flavour.*
Pinot Grigio *Crisp and dry and able to cut through a mix of rich flavours.*
Riesling *Serve very cold. Delicious with fish-based canapés, in particular.*

Meat pâtés and foie gras

Rich foie gras or chicken liver pâté served on crostini is a wonderful combination of textures. Sauternes is the classic accompaniment to foie gras – serve small amounts in tulip-shaped glasses to appreciate the aroma.

Sauternes *A rich, sweet wine able to cope with luxurious foie gras and strong-flavoured pâté. It has acidity also to cleanse the palate. Choose a lighter style such as a Barsac to serve with mild-flavoured pâtés.*

Nuts and salted snacks

Heavily salted snacks will overpower any wine. Choose roasted or lightly salted nuts and plain pretzels and serve with a delicious fortified wine.

Fino sherry *Dry with a nutty flavour itself, this is delicious with nuts.*
Oloroso sherry *Richer than fino; serve with robust-flavoured nuts such as walnuts.*
Sercial Madeira *Dry and acidic, this will enhance most savoury canapés.*

Cheese

Choose wine to suit the texture and flavour of the cheese (see page 117), but if serving the cheese with a strong flavour such as chives, choose a Sancerre or other wine made from the sauvignon grape.

Champagne or sparkling wine *Cream cheese canapés are good with sparkling white wine or Champagne.*
St Emilion *A good mature red brings out the robust flavour of Camembert or hard cheeses.*

Caviar

A luxurious beginning to any party, serve heaped on crostini or blinis. Ideal for greeting wedding guests. You'll need a wine that does justice to this special canapé.

Champagne or sparkling wine *The bubbles work wonderfully with the texture of caviar as it bursts in the mouth. A good-quality vintage Champagne is the most fitting option.*
Champagne cocktail *The sugar and bitters in this classic drink (see page 157) contrast well with caviar.*

Seafood and fish pâtés

If serving freshly shelled seafood such as prawns or lobster, or a delicate fish pâté, choose a light, dry wine to complement its texture and flavour. Avoid serving with lemon, which is acidic and will affect the flavour of the wine.

Pinot grigio *Crisp, dry but light enough not to overpower the delicate fish flavours.*
Riesling *A young Riesling is ideal with seafood canapés, such as tiger prawns or tempura.*

A SELECTION OF CANAPÉS Serve mixed canapés with a refreshing, palate-cleansing, dry white wine or Champagne.

Managing
YOUR COLLECTION

Organising your wine collection is a personal issue. Some people enjoy rummaging through their collections for the right bottle for the occasion; for others, knowing the exact location of the bottle they are seeking is essential. Certainly, if your cellar is sizeable and consists of many different wines, some sort of planning will pay off.

ORGANISING YOUR WINE

Even if you have a small wine collection, labelling your bottles and keeping records can make it easier for you to find your wine and maintain your collection. It is also a requirement of most wine insurance policies.

A simple way of seeing at a glance where wines are located in your cellar is to clearly mark the cases, bins or bottles. On cases or bins filled with the same wine,

fix a piece of card marked with the wine's details. You can identify individual bottles in racks using plastic or paper tags that hang over the necks of the bottles.

An alternative for wine stored in racks – especially useful if your collection has a large variety of wine – is to work out a code for each hole in the rack using a grid system. For example, you can use letters along the top and numbers down the side. If you have more than

one rack, then you will have to designate these too. So you might have a wine in 2B6 which would be found in rack 2 in bin B from the top left and 6 down.

If you have a large amount of wine from only a few regions, each stored separately in your cellar, you can name each rack or stack of bins by that region. You might, for example, have a Bordeaux B6 or a California E4.

RECORDING CELLAR INFORMATION

The purpose of keeping a cellar book (the term "cellar book" applies to information about a wine collection – whether this is stored in a book or in software form) is to allow you to see at a glance exactly what is in your collection; where it can be found; and to monitor stock levels. It can also be an opportunity for you to record your personal tasting notes.

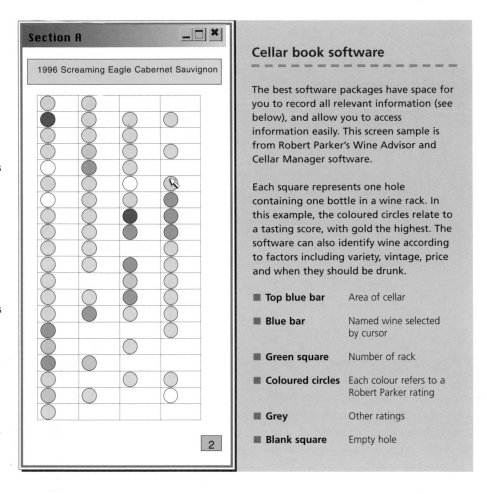

Cellar book software

The best software packages have space for you to record all relevant information (see below), and allow you to access information easily. This screen sample is from Robert Parker's Wine Advisor and Cellar Manager software.

Each square represents one hole containing one bottle in a wine rack. In this example, the coloured circles relate to a tasting score, with gold the highest. The software can also identify wine according to factors including variety, vintage, price and when they should be drunk.

- **Top blue bar**   Area of cellar
- **Blue bar**   Named wine selected by cursor
- **Green square**   Number of rack
- **Coloured circles**   Each colour refers to a Robert Parker rating
- **Grey**   Other ratings
- **Blank square**   Empty hole

Cellar books

Ready-made cellar books range from the basic and practical, to the lavish and ornate. You could have one book for purchase and stock records and a separate, more portable, book to record tasting notes. When selecting or designing a cellar book, make sure that you allocate space for the following:
- *The wine's name; the grape variety or varieties; the country and region of origin; the producer's name; the appellation and vineyard; the vintage; and critics' comments or ratings.*
- *The purchase details, including the date purchased; where you obtained the wine (direct from the producer, wine merchant, auction or gift); the quantity (with a note if the size was other than a standard bottle); and the price paid.*
- *Your storage and stock information – the location of each wine in your cellar and the quantity of each wine.*
- *Consumption records are the most*

personal and flexible item. You could include the date you drank each bottle; tasting notes and/or scores; how the wine is maturing; where and who you were with; and the special occasion or food that accompanied the wine.

Computer software

There are many cellar management software programs available on the market, which can either be purchased as a CD-ROM or downloaded from the internet. All are based on a spreadsheet format with fields for recording information about your wine, with an explanation of how to complete the fields. Some are linked to vintage charts and tasting notes from well-known critics. You can also buy regular vintage updates and incorporate them into your system. It is a good idea to download a trial example from the internet before buying.

Troubleshooting

If you have followed the rules for creating ideal conditions for your wine, you should sleep soundly at night, dreaming of the moment when you will uncork a perfectly matured bottle. Though unlikely, nightmare scenarios such as burglary, flooding and insect infestations are possible, however, so be aware and know how to rectify problems quickly.

OUT OF CONDITION

Monitoring temperature and humidity and keeping an eye on light levels in your cellar are very important if your wine is going to age properly and not become damaged. Take regular readings of the temperature and humidity levels, and keep a clear record, so that if problems start to occur, you will be forewarned. So what should you look out for?

Warning signs

A visible indication of damage to your wine often means that the damage is too far gone to be reversed. If you notice any of the following signs of trouble in your collection, take immediate action to salvage unaffected bottles and make adjustments to your cellar conditions:

■ *Seepage around the wine capsule or increased air space between the cork and the wine – known as ullage – means that your wine has begun to evaporate and may be at risk from oxidization. This could be caused by an excessively high temperature in your cellar. It could also be an indication of low humidity, especially if the cork appears to have dried out.*

■ *Protruding corks may be a sign that the wine has frozen, forcing the cork out of the bottle. If the temperature surrounding your wine collection does drop too low, raising it very gradually may prevent further damage (see pages 44–5).*

■ *Mouldy labels are a sign of high humidity. The wine itself will not be affected, but if the problem is left unchecked, the mould might spread and render the labels illegible, which will affect re-sale value.*

■ *Discoloured, brown wine may indicate that a wine has been exposed to sunlight or a strong electric light. Discolouration indicates oxidization and the flavour of the wine will be ruined. White wines in clear glass bottles are particularly sensitive. To avoid this, see page 44 for ways to block out light.*

POTENTIAL PROBLEMS *This wine collection could face problems caused by wine being stored upright, in cardboard boxes directly on the floor and being wrapped in tissue paper.*

BOTTLE PROTECTION

If you live in a humid area, or an area at risk from flood, you can protect the labels on valuable bottles. Bottle neck capsules are not airtight, so if you

Use hair spray or water-proofing spray to protect labels. Test on the back label first to check for absorption.

think your wine is at risk from temperature changes or insect infestation, see below:

To protect both the cork and the label, wrap bottles tightly using clingfilm or bubble wrap.

re-corking old wine

If you have wines capable of ageing for several decades, you should consider having them re-corked after 30 years. However good your cellar conditions are, corks gradually shrivel, and may even disintegrate, so replacing them will protect the wine for longer. The procedure is best left to an expert or the original winery (check with your wine merchant for further details).

The old cork is carefully removed and the wine is topped up with the same wine from a younger vintage. A small dose of sulphur dioxide is added before finally re-corking with a new cork.

BURGLARY

Expensive collections of fine wines are big business for burglars. If you have a large selection of sought-after wines, make sure that your cellar has special security, such as alarmed doors. You will also need to make sure that your wine is properly insured.

FLOODING

A basement is the part of your home that is most likely to suffer in the event of a flood, so if you live in a flood-risk area, keep your wine collection as high as possible, ideally not in the basement or underground, and ensure that the wine is in sturdy racks off the floor.

A mild flood is not a problem, as long as you de-humidify the room afterwards. If it is a serious flood that reaches the wine, the wine might float out of the racks, and could break. The most likely damage will be that the labels will be unreadable and may come off. Keeping good records could help identify the bottles, but their re-sale value will be severely reduced.

INSECT INFESTATIONS

It has been known for weevils or beetles to eat into corks, reducing their efficacy, and letting in air. Check that the capsules on your bottles are intact and hang an insect strip in your cellar to ward off possible infestations of insects. If you live in a high-risk area, you could wrap your bottles (see above).

INSURANCE

A small collection can be included as part of a home contents insurance policy, but you should contact your insurer to check details – many will only insure for fire or theft and not for accidental damage. Make sure that the policy pays out replacement cost rather than original cost in case of a loss.

If your wine is worth a lot of money, it may be wise to take out specialist insurance. These brokers usually have strict conditions, but you can be confident that they have an excellent understanding of the wine business. Most policies will insist on an initial valuation, proof of purchase and regular valuations thereafter. Insurance that includes accidental damage will also require your wine cellar to have the right temperature and humidity levels (see page 44) for wine storage. Up-to-date, detailed records of the contents of your wine collection are also essential (see pages 54–5). If you have difficulty finding a specialist insurer, try asking in your local wine merchants, or in the nearest wine storage warehouse.

WHEN IS WINE READY TO

Drink?

Tasting a wine as it matures is one of the greatest joys of owning a cellar. It is better to drink wine too early than too late, but it is largely a matter of personal taste at what maturity you enjoy a wine. A quality red Bordeaux, for example, is generally enjoyed by typical French drinkers earlier than by traditional British claret lovers.

WHAT DEFINES MATURE WINE

Only wines with sufficient complexity will improve with ageing. Some wines are meant to be drunk young and fresh (see pages 30–31). A wine at perfect maturity is in complete balance and has a complexity of flavour, both on the nose (smell) and the palate (taste), while retaining a long finish. However, personal taste varies widely. Some people prefer a wine that has lots of structure, others prefer wine once it has developed a softer, smoother taste. In addition, not everyone enjoys the flavours that develop in a wine with age.

Good timing

Assessing how long a wine is capable of ageing is one of the most difficult aspects of tasting, and experience is everything. This is why many wine lovers rely on professionals to give them guidance in their decisions on when is the right time to open a bottle. Any good producer or merchant who sells fine wines destined for ageing should provide a guide to their optimum drinking period. There are also plenty of specialist wine collector magazines and "tip sheets" available that will guide you.

This chart features a selection of fine, age-worthy wine styles from around the world. It shows the average time span for selected wines to mature after bottling (some are not released for sale for some years after bottling). It also indicates when the wine will begin to decline.

Within the "Ready to drink" period, the wine will develop, gaining complexity until it reaches its peak, provided it is stored well. The length of time a wine takes to mature will vary from producer to producer and also between vintages.

Reaching the age of maturity

Examples of wines	Bottling date (years after production)	Ageing period (years after bottling)	Ready to drink (years after bottling)	In decline (years after bottling)
1st Growth Pauillac (red Bordeaux)	2½	2½–15	15–30	30+
Premier Cru Côtes de Nuits (red Burgundy)	1½	1½–8	8–20	20+
Top Estate red Hermitage (Rhône)	2	2–8	8–25	25+
Californian Cabernet Sauvignon Reserve	2	2–5	5–20	20+
Chianti Classico Riserva (Tuscany, Italy)	3	3–6	6–18	18+
Barolo Riserva (Piedmont, Italy)	5	5–15	15–30	30+
Rioja Gran Reserva (Spain)	3	3–5	5–20	20+
Grand Cru Côtes de Beaune (white Burgundy)	1½	1½–4	4–15	15+
German Rheingau Riesling Auslese	1	1–5	5–25	25+
Vintage port	2	2–15	15–35	35+

Judging maturity

Appearance White wine loses any green tinges and turns a deeper yellow, towards gold or even amber. A brown colour, however, is indicative of oxidization. Red wine colour changes are more obvious. The colour at the rim of the glass turns first from purple to red, then towards garnet, and eventually brown. The intensity of colour in a red gradually fades with age and eventually the core of the wine in the glass turns towards garnet and brown, like the rim. An older red wine may well form a sediment, which could end up in your glass.

BOTTLE SHOCK *Even white wine intended to be drunk young needs time to mature. After the bottling process, wine goes through a period of shock and fine wines are held in the winery for couple of months before being released.*

Smell The smell of a young wine, often described as its aroma, is primarily of fruit, usually associated with a particular grape variety. As the wine ages, secondary aromas develop, sometimes known as the bouquet. This owes more to how the wine was made – smells of spice, for example, for a red aged in oak. A mature, fine wine has such complexity of flavours on the nose that it becomes almost impossible to describe. Each time you smell it, a different flavour emerges, as if layers of flavour have developed.

Palate A fine wine, destined for ageing, can taste disjointed or unbalanced when young. The components – sweetness, acidity, tannin, alcohol and flavours – may seem separated. As the wine matures, these components start to marry. In the process, the flavours sometimes disappear for a while, in a stage which wine tasters often describe as "dumb" or "closed". Finally, everything comes together, so that the wine tastes in complete harmony or balance with perfect structure and flavour.

Length This is one of the best ways to judge a wine's maturity. Good length, when the flavour remains in the mouth for a couple of minutes after you have swallowed or spat out the wine, is indicative of a wine that will age well – provided it has good structure and fruit. As the wine ages, the length becomes shorter, and with time, the flavours will simply disappear.

cellarmaster tips

■ It can be very disappointing to keep a wine for many years, only to find that it is past its best when you taste it. To avoid this, buy at least two cases of a wine that you want to age. Open a bottle soon after you have purchased it, to taste it young. Record tasting notes. To monitor how the wine is developing, open further bottles every 6 months or so, according to the recommended drinking window. You are unlikely to drink more than 12 bottles in this way, and will then be able to indulge in a further 12 at the perfect point of maturity.

■ Some mature wines will have developed a sediment or deposit of solid matter by the time they are ready. At least one day before serving an old bottle, take the bottle out of its rack and stand it upright to allow the sediment to settle. Decant carefully (see pages 128–9).

■ Wine in half-bottles ages more quickly than in full bottles, and wine in magnums and larger format bottles ages more slowly.

Wine with
FISH AND SHELLFISH

The natural choice for fish is a white wine, but there are so many kinds of fish and so many ways in which you can cook them, that you'll need to think hard about which wine to choose. Bear in mind also the other ingredients that are going to accompany the fish.

Oily fish

This includes tuna, sardines and mackerel. They have a meaty texture and big flavours, and are delicious chargrilled. You'll need a fairly robust wine that will complement the meaty texture.

Beaujolais Villages *A fruity wine that has the right amount of acid to suit oily fish.*
Muscadet *Particularly successful with mackerel.*

Smoked fish

Smokiness varies – from creamy smoked salmon to a strong smoked mackerel. Few wines have the potency to withstand a strongly smoked fish.

Champagne *For smoked salmon, there is nothing better.*
Fino and manzanilla sherries *For rich smoked fish, these can be good partners.*
Mosel *The lightness and crispness of a fine quality Mosel works beautifully with smoked, peppered mackerel.*

Freshwater fish

Clean-tasting freshwater fish, such as trout or salmon, can be baked, grilled or poached. They need flavoursome white wines.

Chablis *This is a fresh, earthy wine, perfect for enhancing the flavours of a simply cooked trout or salmon.*
Riesling *Go for a light-bodied type that will allow the flavours of the fish to shine through.*
Gewürztraminer *Its spicy flavour works well if your trout is served with rich accompaniments.*

Shellfish

There is a variety of shellfish and a great deal depends on how you are cooking and serving it.

Gewürztraminer *Grilled lobster drizzled with olive oil needs a fruity, spicy wine.*
Red Rioja *Shrimp or prawns cooked in a creamy sauce will benefit from the richness of a Rioja.*
Riesling *For crab, you'll need a refreshing white wine.*

Molluscs

Oysters and scallops have very delicate flavours and a distinctive consistency that can be very difficult to match with wine. Go for the lighter whites.

Chardonnay *Choose an unwooded type that won't overpower the subtle flavours.*
Pinot Gris *If you are serving scallops cooked with butter, the spiciness will work beautifully.*

Saltwater fish

Cod, haddock and other saltwater fish are often best served lightly poached with a squeeze of lemon to bring out the flavour, or, classically, deep fried. Do not overwhelm with lemon, else the wine will clash.

Chardonnay *An oaked Chardonnay will work well with the flavour of the fish and the lemon.*
White Burgundy *For deep-fried cod or haddock, you'll need a wine with oakiness, but sufficiently acidic to cleanse the palate.*

GRILLED MACKEREL WITH ROASTED VEGETABLES Serve oily fish such as mackerel with Muscadet or Beaujolais Villages.

3

We all know how to drink wine, but tasting it can be another matter. In this chapter we take the mystique out of the tasting sequence, and explain how you can assess a wine with confidence. We take you through each stage in detail – looking, smelling and tasting – and list the observations that wine professionals make, and that you will encounter. This includes how to distinguish a good wine from a faulty wine, how to identify the main grape varieties and how to develop your tasting skills.

We look also at tasting opportunities, from shop-based tastings to wine holidays and clubs, and the appropriate etiquette at each. This includes ordering and tasting wine in a restaurant, choosing wine for a function and the correct etiquette for tasting.

tasting

wine

THE *Tasting* SEQUENCE

There is a fair amount of mystique surrounding the tasting sequence employed by wine professionals, but in fact it is very easy to master. The three steps of assessing a wine – in the glass, on the nose and on the palate – enable you to appreciate fully the complexity of a wine. We explain each step in detail over the following pages.

TASTING VERSUS DRINKING

Everyone knows how to drink wine, but tasting wine requires a little more thought. Most wine has subtleties of aroma, taste and texture that you cannot appreciate fully when you simply drink a glass of wine in a social situation. When you are in a bar or restaurant, there may also be environmental factors that can distract you from the wine, such as tobacco smoke and perfume smells, or the wine might be the wrong temperature to show off its intricacies.

Tasting wine is all about taking time to think about what you are drinking. If you give yourself a few minutes to focus on a wine – to look at it, smell it and then taste it – you will be able to experience all of its nuances and enjoy the complexity of the wine entirely. You will be doing justice to the wine and to yourself. Furthermore, as you slow down the process to savour what you are drinking, you will also be able to expand your knowledge and understanding of individual wines.

THE THREE STEPS

The tasting sequence has been used for many years by wine enthusiasts. It is the logical way of approaching a wine: by sight, smell and taste. The three steps are:

In the glass This is your opportunity to look at the wine when poured in a glass. By assessing the colour and texture of the wine, you can start to make deductions about its origins, age and possible flavour.

On the nose By smelling the wine in the glass, you can begin to unravel the layers of flavour in the wine.

On the palate In the last stage, you taste the wine, and roll it around your mouth and all over your tongue, to get a feel for the wine.

IN THE GLASS *Take a good look at the wine in a glass to note the colour, texture and body.*

ON THE NOSE *Smell the wine to note its aromas, and to give you an idea of the flavours to come.*

ON THE PALATE *Finally, taste the wine to feel the wine in your mouth, and to taste its flavours.*

TASTING TIPS

If you want to get the most out of the tasting sequence and extend your knowledge of wine, bear the following factors in mind before you start:

■ Make sure that the wine is at the right temperature (see pages 114–15). If the wine is too warm or too cold, your perceptions of its flavours may be altered.

■ Make sure that you use an uncut, clear glass so you can see the wine clearly (see pages 130–1).

■ Swirl your glass to release the aroma of the wine before you smell it.

■ Taste the wine before you consume any food, to get an untainted perception of its flavours.

■ Sip your wine slowly so that it coats your whole mouth, and think about what flavours you can taste.

■ Start a tasting diary of wines you have enjoyed.

■ Extend your perception of smells by taking note of the smells around you.

Analysing your taste

Think about which wines you like the most, and try to consider the reasons why. Do you like white wine because it is crisp and dry? Or rich and honey-flavoured? Do you prefer red wine because it has mellower flavours? By thinking about which wine flavours you like, you will start to see a pattern, and begin to discern your preferences. This will help you to identify some of the characteristics of different wines.

Getting started

Next time you taste a glass of wine, take note of your initial thoughts. Would you be able to identify the same wine another time? Try to make distinctions about the wine that will help you to identify it, or to describe it to someone else. You could buy wine that a well-respected wine critic recommends, and see if you agree with his or her tasting notes. Likewise, do your ideas relate to the tasting notes on the bottle? It is very likely that you will disagree with some of the notes – we all have different tastes and preferences – but making the comparisons will provide you with useful practice in the art of tasting.

ORGANISED TASTINGS *There are many opportunities for tasting wines, from large-scale festivals, to informal tastings held by a local wine shop.*

STEP 1: IN THE *Glass*

The first step in assessing a wine is to take a good look at it. You can start to deduce a lot of information from the colour and consistency of a wine, such as where the wine might have come from, how old it is and what the wine might taste like. This is also the first opportunity to check for potential faults.

COLOUR

Wine is often identified by its colour – red, white or rosé – but there's a great deal more to it than that. Red wines can be opaque and almost black, or they can be the colour of dark rosé. White wine can be water-white, or a deep yellow. Rosé wine can range from the palest salmon pink, to quite dark pink. There are also fortified wines to consider. Sherry, for example, is classed as a white wine, since it is made from white grapes, but its colours can vary from the pale colour of fino to the near-black of an old oloroso. Port (technically a red wine) can be the deep black of a

young vintage wine, or the nut-brown of an aged tawny. Even faced with a vast range of wine colours, we can draw useful conclusions about a wine by looking at it.

TEXTURE AND BODY

Swirl the wine around the glass, then allow it to settle. You will see droplets forming on the inside of the glass and then running down back into the wine. Often called "legs", these are sometimes taken to be a sign of high quality. In fact, they are just a sign of high alcohol – they are formed because of the relative evaporation rates of water and alcohol. A wine with high alcohol is likely to feel "bigger" and richer in the mouth.

WHAT TO LOOK OUT FOR

All wine should look bright in the glass. If a wine looks cloudy, then there is something wrong with it, but very few wines these days suffer from the problem.

With age, white wines become darker and eventually take on a brownish tint. When they get to this stage they are generally too old to drink – they will have lost their fruity, fresh taste.

When a red wine loses so much colour with age that it takes on a brownish tint, the wine is probably well past its best.

Wine throws two kinds of deposits in bottle and, although harmless, either kind spoils the look of your wine if it gets into your glass.

Tartrate crystals are small, white, powdery crystals of harmless tartaric acid. Most producers chill wines to low temperatures before bottling to make the tartrates precipitate out; this is the reason they so seldom appear in bottles.

Red wines that have been left to mature in bottle for many years often throw a dark deposit composed of tannins and colour.

DARK TO LIGHT Ageing red wine in oak barrels makes it mellow, with a softer colour. The bright colour of a young Cabernet Sauvignon (left) fades to a brick–garnet shade (right) after being aged in the bottle for 25 years.

LOOKING AT COLOUR

1 Hold the glass against a white background – a tablecloth or a piece of white paper is ideal.

2 Swirl the glass gently and watch for legs as the wine runs around the glass. Look closely at the colour of the wine from the rim inwards.

CHECKING FOR DEPOSITS

1 At least one day before opening a bottle of wine that has been ageing, stand it upright. Any sediment or deposits will settle in the bottom of the bottle.

2 If you notice any sediment, decant the wine, taking care not to get sediment in the decanter (see page 129).

Vintage port is particularly known for this, so it is usually decanted (see pages 128–9). This deposit or crust makes the wine look muddy, and may also give it a bitter flavour. It's far better to leave it in the bottle.

BUBBLES

The appearance of the bubbles in a sparkling wine can give you a clue about its quality. Champagne and other sparkling wines made by the "traditional method", or *Méthode Traditionelle*, have a stream of fine, small bubbles. Sparkling wine made by other methods, such as tank fermentation, sometimes known as Charmat or Cuve Close, may have bigger bubbles.

COMPARING LEGS This wine above doesn't have legs, but the prominent legs on the wine below show that it is high in alcohol.

Some wines, such as Portuguese Vinho Verde, are bottled with the addition of just a little carbon dioxide under pressure. When you drink these wines, you feel just a light prickle on the tongue and they may leave a thin layer of small bubbles clinging to the inside of the bowl of the glass.

FORTIFIED WINES

Fino sherry is the palest of all fortified wines, in spite of having been aged for several years in oak barrels. It owes its light colour to a yeast called flor, which grows on the surface of the wine in the barrel and keeps it fresh in flavour and pale in colour. Oloroso sherries are darker than fino sherries (see page 163).

Port varies in colour according to the different blends and ageing processes. A vintage port that has been bottled young, will have a very rich, deep colour – almost black, with just some pink showing at the rim. As it ages in the bottle its colour will fade slowly. Tawny port, unlike vintage, spends many years in oak barrels before being bottled, and so has already lost much of its colour by the time it is bottled. It has a mellow, nutty colour.

WHAT TO LOOK FOR

A pale colour in a white indicates a wine that is very young and was bottled early, without any ageing in wood. Soave, for example, is almost colourless at the rim. A very pale white wine should taste fresh, young and well-balanced. Leaving a white wine to age in oak barrels, on the other hand, tends to darken its colour.

A light-coloured red may be a sign of a cool climate. Darker colours in reds, as in whites, may indicate warmer regions. Some red grape varieties yield lighter coloured wines than others – pinot noir, for example. Other grape varieties are capable of producing wines of a variety of colours, depending on the climate in which they are grown and the production process used. Californian zinfandel, for example, produces every range of red from light pink through to almost black.

Dark reds may indicate a warm climate, and – quite the opposite of white wines – richness of colour can also be evidence of youth in a red.

MERLOT This is a French Merlot. It is relatively light in colour, indicating that it may have come from a cool climate.

RIOJA This northern Spanish red has a darker colour – it is probably quite young.

SHIRAZ This is an Australian Syrah. The rich ruby red shows that it is young, and comes from a hot climate.

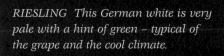

RIESLING This German white is very pale with a hint of green – typical of the grape and the cool climate.

GEWÜRZTRAMINER The stronger and slightly golden colour are tell-tale signs of this rich wine.

SEMILLON Darker still, the rich, deep yellow of this French white indicates a mature wine.

STEP 2: ON THE *Nose*

This is where serious tasters really get down to business. The nose of a wine – a term that simply means the smell – tells you just as much as the flavour. Even if you're just drinking, rather than tasting properly, it's worth spending a few moments "on the nose". Missing out on the nose means losing out on much of the flavour and subtlety of a wine.

WHAT DOES THE NOSE TELL YOU?

One sniff of a wine can reveal a great deal about it – its grape variety, how it was made and how it was matured. Experienced tasters can tell almost everything they need to know about a wine from the nose alone.

When you smell wine, you pick up so many layers of aroma, or aromatic compounds, that it can be difficult to categorise them. Compare the aromas with other familiar smells – such as fruit and vegetables (see pages 72–3) – to help you to describe an aroma and describe it to others.

Is the wine faulty?

The most important thing to discover at this stage is whether the wine is in good condition. Wine should smell clean, whatever other smells are there. If it smells

of wet cardboard, rotten eggs, burnt rubber, vinegary or musty, it is faulty. It may be oxidized, have cork taint or be turning to vinegar (see pages 80–81) – whatever the reason, it won't be very nice to drink.

Dumb or closed wines

Some wines have very little nose, and no matter how hard you try, you can define nothing from them. Tasters describe such wines as "dumb" or "closed". Sometimes youth is the cause – some wines go through a dumb phase before reaching full maturity. Or the wine might be too cold, or it might need to breathe for a while before you taste it again.

AROMA AND BOUQUET

These two terms are often used interchangeably, though in fact they mean different things. Aroma is the smell of a young wine, and is also used generically when discussing the smell of wine. Bouquet is the smell of a mature wine.

Bouquet embraces the physical and chemical changes that take place as wine ages. These smells are harder to describe than the simple fresh, fruity aromas of young wine. White wines often develop a smell and flavour of honey over time; reds become mellower, and gain depth of smell and flavour.

As you learn to distinguish between the two, you will be able to judge the age and maturity of a wine from the nose.

Become aroma aware

This couldn't be simpler – just take note of the smells around you. You may already breathe in the aroma of strawberries or peaches or freshly ground coffee, just for the pleasure of it. Next time you slice a green pepper, take note of the smell. The same goes for flowers, leaves, cut grass, cooked apple or the smell of a well-aged leather chair. Note the smell of coal smoke, freshly laundered linen, cardboard or forest undergrowth on a wet day. Remember them for when you want to describe a wine.

Fruit and flower smells

Natural aromas of fruits, flowers and vegetation often come from the variety of grape used in the wine – both in red and white wine. They can be the most evocative ways of

---

NOSING STEP-BY-STEP

1 Fill the glass no more than one-third full, or to where the bowl starts to fill out. If you fill the glass any more, you risk spilling the wine when you swirl it.

2 Take the glass by the stem or by the base. This allows you to tilt the glass when looking at it, and to swirl the glass. If you prefer to swirl on a flat surface (see below), hold at the base.

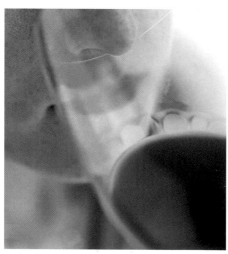

3 Swirl the glass gently in a circular motion to release the aromatic compounds in the wine. Take care not to swirl it so it spills over the rim. You can place the glass on a firm surface for extra stability, or swirl in the air.

4 Tilt the glass towards you and place your nose inside the bowl. Your nose should not touch the wine. Take one deep sniff and remove your nose from the glass to consider the aromas. Alternatively, take 3 or 4 short sniffs.

describing the aromas of a wine, so when you next taste a wine that you think is "fruity", try to think about exactly which fruits you can taste – is it tropical fruits, berry fruits, cooked fruits or citrus fruits? And is it sharp lemon, bitter lemon or tangy lemon?

Wines can smell of flowers, too, although it is seldom as easy to pin down a particular flower smell. An aroma of roses is not uncommon on wines from the gewürztraminer grape, but for most wines, a vague impression of general spring flowers is far more usual.

Curiously, the one fruit smell that you seldom find in wine is that of grapes. The exception is wine from the muscat grape, however, which is reminiscent of fresh, aromatic, dessert grapes.

Oak and wood smells

Smells of vanilla, butter and toast – on red wines and on white – usually result when a wine has been aged in oak barrels, for example, Chardonnay. If the wine has been aged in oak for too long, the wine may smell like a timber yard, with the fruit overwhelmed by the smell of oak. The fruit may emerge again as the wine ages, or it may not. Smells of spices such as cinnamon and cloves also come from oak.

Different sorts of oak impart different smells and flavours to wine: US oak gives a full vanilla flavour, while French oak is more subtle. German oak is spicy; Portuguese oak, chocolatey.

The type of oak used for maturing a wine is the choice of the winemaker, but most prefer French or US oak. The latter imparts most flavour and is used for wines with the weight to stand up to it, such as Chardonnay from the Napa valley.

Crispness

A very crisp, clean aroma may indicate that a wine hasn't been aged in oak barrels at all – many wines are not. A lot of winemakers prefer to keep their young wines in stainless steel vats until bottling, to preserve the crispness of youth.

Even if a wine smells crisp, it is impossible to determine the level of acidity, or tannin, by its smell alone. The most effective way of assessing this is by tasting it (see pages 74–7).

HOW TO DESCRIBE THE NOSE

The most commonly found smells are outlined above, but there are general comments that you can make that are also widely used:

Lacking fruit A wine that doesn't smell of fruit. It tends to imply that the wine is either very young or is very old and has lost its aroma completely.

Pungent Having a strong, tangy smell. It can be used as a complimentary term. Sauvignon Blanc is often described as having a pungent aroma.

Aromatic This refers to any kind of strong, pronounced smell in a wine. It is most often used when a wine has a particularly flowery scent.

Powerful nose Used to describe a wine with a very strong smell. Again, usually complimentary.

Use the wheel

The Aroma Wheel (opposite) was created and developed by Ann Noble as a result of her research into sensory evaluation of wine at the University of California. The wheel provides a list of key words that can be used to pin down and define a multitude of aromas found in wine. It is used around the world and provides a standard by which every taster can understand the complex aromas of wine in the same way. The wheel can be used to narrow down a general observation to a specific term. It can be employed as a detailed foundation of terminology, but many tasters develop their own terms as they gain confidence.

You can use the aroma wheel to develop your own tasting skills and vocabulary. Start at the inner section of the wheel and from a general observation about the wine you are tasting – "fruity", for example – you can narrow down the taste to a type of fruit, such as "dried", and then further to a specific fruit, such as "prune".

SENSORY PERCEPTION Take note of the aromas around you, such as a leather chair, a vase of flowers or sliced fruit. Remember how these smell and add them to your aroma vocabulary.

The aroma wheel

The Aroma Wheel © 1990 A.C. Noble. Coloured laminated copies of the wine aroma wheel may be obtained from Ann C. Noble at The Department of Viticulture and Enology, University of California, Davis, CA USA 95616.

STEP 3: ON THE *Palate*

This is the stage at which you confirm, and learn more about, what the first two stages have told you about the wine in your glass. All the richness or delicacy of flavour promised by the colour and the aroma should be here. Once you have taken a mouthful of wine, swirled it around and swallowed or spat it out, it will have revealed all it can.

SMELLING WITH YOUR MOUTH

Our experience tells us that we "taste" the flavour of raspberries or oak or apples in wine. The only ingredients that go into wine are grapes, however, and perhaps a hint of the wood from the barrel they were aged in. What you taste are actually aromatic compounds from the fermented grapes. The compounds are vaporised in your mouth and your brain registers them as smells. In effect, you're smelling with your mouth.

The tongue registers only four basic flavours – sweetness at the front, sourness or acidity at the sides, saltiness (a flavour not usually found in wine) in between and bitterness at the back. By moving the wine around and over your tongue you allow yourself to taste all of the aspects and appreciate all of the flavours of the wine. When you take wine into your mouth in a tasting, the wine usually reaches the front of your tongue first, so you taste the wine's sweetness first, sourness and acidity next, followed by bitterness. Our mouths can also interpret the substance and texture of a wine (see pages 76–7).

Sweetness

Unfermented grape sugar provides the flavour of sweetness in wine. Dessert wines such as Sauternes and fortified wines such as Malmsey Madeira have high levels of unfermented sugar (called "residual sugar"). Even Californian Chardonnay, however, which we perceive as dry, often has several grams of residual sugar per litre. In a dry wine, like a Chardonnay, the other flavours, such as acidity, counter the sweetness, so that the overriding sensation is dry rather than sweet. In tasting terms, the opposite of "sweet" is "dry".

TASTING STEP-BY-STEP

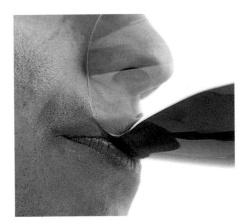

1 Take a sip of wine. You should take enough to coat your tongue, but your mouth should not feel full. Hold the wine in your mouth.

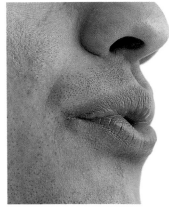

2 Purse your lips. Draw air in through your lips over your tongue. The idea is to pull air through the wine and release its volatile compounds.

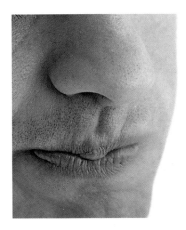

3 Roll the wine around to coat the whole mouth. Think about the flavours of the wine, its texture and how it feels in your mouth.

4 When you have learned all you can from the wine, either swallow it, or if tasting a large quantity of wine, spit it into an appropriate receptacle.

---

critic's tips

- If the order of wines is not determined for them, many people prefer to taste white wine before red and young wine before mature. A young wine that tastes fresh and crisp on its own can taste lean and acidic if you taste it after a much older one. Similarly, a light wine can taste insipid after a rich, heavy one.
- If you are tasting a number of wines, spit them out after tasting. If you consume alcohol, your perceptions will diminish.
- Cleanse your palate between tastings by eating a plain, dry cracker or by rinsing your mouth thoroughly with water.

palate

Strictly speaking, the word "palate" refers to the roof of the mouth. If a taster says "This wine has a palate of oak and honey", however, he or she is referring to the taste of the wine.

Acidity

A wine that tastes "crisp" has high levels of acidity; one that tastes weak and flabby has low levels. Acidity is one of the elements that preserves wine while it ages; young whites, in particular, which are destined for long bottle ageing, can seem extremely high in acidity when they are young. Acidity levels do not fall with time, but wines gradually begin to taste softer and rounder as the edge is taken off. The higher the residual sugar in a wine, the more acidity it needs to make it balanced.

A light dry wine can taste more acidic than a sweet wine, even if the sweet wine actually has far more acidity. Sourness in a wine is a fault.

Bitterness

Not a flavour you want or expect to find in wine, bitterness should not be confused with a feeling of astringency, which comes from tannin. If a wine tastes unpleasantly bitter, it might be a sign of a fault, and could be turning to vinegar. Vinegar-flavoured wine is irrevocably faulty. Occasionally, you may detect a touch of bitter oak flavour in the wine, which means that the oak barrel in which it was aged has not been properly seasoned, but this is uncommon.

Striking a balance

Put all these elements together in one wine, and if the result is to be a harmonious, delicious wine, balance is crucial. As a general rule, the parts of the wine that give it what is called "backbone" – tannin and acidity – need to be balanced by fruit and sweetness. A wine that is all fruit or sweetness will be flabby; one that is all tannin and acidity will be "tough" or "hard".

TASTE SENSATIONS

Is the wine creamy, silky and velvety, or astringent and drying? How does it feel on your tongue? When you've swallowed or spat out a wine, take a few moments to note how long the flavour lasts.

Tannin

This is one of the essential components of red wine. Technically, tannins are a group of compounds that come from the skins, pips and stalks of red grapes. You can detect tannin as a drying, astringent sensation that coats your mouth as you taste a wine. Test what tannin tastes like by sipping strong, cold tea.

The amount of tannin that you can detect in a wine is a useful indicator of its maturity. Young red wine has more aggressive tannin than mature red wine – one of the results of ageing is that the tannin content of the wine becomes softer, and the wine tastes smoother and mellower.

One of the main aims of red wine makers these days, however, is to produce young wines that have rich, velvety textures. Wine tasters comment on the "ripe tannins" in such wines. "Green tannins" are the opposite – drying and harsh on the palate.

Tasting a number of tannic red wines can be extremely hard work – the tannin builds up in your mouth and makes it progressively harder to assess each wine. Sip and spit some water between wines to wash your mouth out or eat a plain, dry cracker.

Body

This term refers to the impression of weight and size of the wine in your mouth. Wine can seem heavier according to the amount of alcohol in the wine – the more alcohol, the fuller the mouthfeel. The fashion today is for red wine to have lots of body, so many wine producers have increased the alcohol levels.

Length

The flavour of a simple wine disappears very quickly from the mouth once you have swallowed it, whereas the taste of a fine wine will linger, often for up to a minute. This aftertaste is known as the "length" of the wine. If the wine is young, or of poor quality, it will not last very long on the palate, but if it is good quality or mature, the flavour will stick around. At an organised

FLAVOURS AND AROMAS Look for notes of fruits, herbs and vegetation as you taste a wine.

DESCRIBING YOUR FINDINGS When you are tasting several wines, it can be difficult to articulate your thoughts clearly. Use the tasting terms (right) to help you out.

tasting, you may hear other tasters say appreciatively, "good length" or "very long" after they have tasted a wine. Conversely, "short" is a dismissive comment.

FLAVOUR FAMILIES

You will often hear wines referred to according to groups of flavours. The main groups you will encounter are fruit, earth, minerals, spice and wood. These are generic descriptive terms that cover a wide range of flavours, and are a useful starting point when describing wines. They refer to both red and white wines.

glossary of tasting terms

Austere Lean, hard, without charm or fruit. Might just be too young.

Beefy Rich, weighty, solid. Applied to red wine only.

Coarse Lacks elegance.

Complex Reveals many different characteristics.

Depth Has many layers of flavour.

Elegant A well-balanced, delicious wine.

Fat Often applied to sweet wines to denote a full mouthfeel.

Finesse Very elegant.

Firm Good acidic or tannic structure.

Forward Mature for its age.

Hard Overwhelming tannin or acidity.

Heavy Lots of alcohol and perhaps not enough freshness and acidity.

Herbaceous Grassy, leafy flavours.

Jammy Stewed fruit flavours. Lacks freshness.

Spritz Light prickle on the tongue from a touch of carbon dioxide in the wine. Found in young, light whites, often to their advantage.

Stalky A lean, somewhat green flavour that comes from vine stems. Found in red wines.

Stewed Tastes cooked. Think of stewed apple compared to fresh.

Steely High acidity, firmness. Applied to white wines, often young ones that will benefit from further ageing.

Structure The balance of the basic elements – fruit, acidity, sweetness and tannin. A wine has a good, firm structure, or a poor, weak structure.

Supple Silky, smooth, no awkward edges.

Thin Lacking roundness.

Vegetal Cabbage-like. Mature Burgundy, red and white, can be deliciously vegetal; in many other wines a cabbage-like flavour is a fault.

Zesty Fresh, lively.

MEAT

Every meat has its own distinctive flavour, but the way in which it is prepared and cooked has a great impact on how that flavour manifests itself at the dinner table. You need to consider all of these aspects when you are choosing your wine.

Beef

Whether you are serving plain rump steak or a complex casserole, you'll need a rich, robust red wine that will pick up the distinctive meaty flavour of beef.

Bordeaux *Rich, red and full of flavour, this is the classic partner for a juicy steak.*
Burgundy *In a casserole, the texture of the beef is much softer, so a lighter-bodied, milder red is required.*

Pork

Pork can be cooked and served in a variety of ways and your cooking methods will certainly dictate the type of wine that you will need.

Chianti *For marinaded, barbecued pork, choose a wine that will complement the charcoal flavours.*
Rioja *Roast pork requires a full-bodied red, such as Rioja.*
Valpolicella *If you are serving pork with sweetened apple sauce, this Italian wine will be delicious.*

Lamb

Roast young lamb is far different in texture and more subtle in flavour than mature lamb. Choose your accompanying wine accordingly. Be sparing with mint sauce as it will clash with most wines.

Grenache *A blend with Syrah is ideal for a roast spring lamb dish.*
Bordeaux *A Pomerol from Bordeaux is best with older lamb. It has a deep, rich flavour, but relatively low tannin and acidity.*

Veal

You can judge veal by the colour of the meat. The whiter the meat, the more tender and delicately flavoured it is likely to be, and it will need a lighter wine.

Vouvray *Fine dry and off-dry whites are good with white veal.*
Bordeaux *A rich red brings out the more defined flavours of darker veal.*
Soave *This light dry white works well if the veal is served with a creamy white wine sauce.*

Sausages

Choose your wine according to the kind of meat and the nature of the sausage mixture. A heavily spiced sausage might be difficult to match with wine.

Shiraz *Very full-bodied and ripe in flavour, this will work well with most types of sausage.*
Côtes de Rhône *A hearty red is the best accompaniment to a good, flavoursome sausage.*

Cold meats

Salami and other preserved meats are often very strongly flavoured and will need a rich red. The fat content of meats is more apparent when cold, so choose a more acidic wine than usual.

Rhône *Aromatic and full-bodied wines from this region are great with all cold meats.*
Pinot Noir *Choose a Californian or New World variety for maximum compatibility.*

GRILLED STEAK WITH TRUFFLE Serve a rich meat dish with a robust red such as Burgundy.

RECOGNIZING *Good and Bad* WINE

Today's winemaking methods mean that even the most basic, inexpensive wine can be perfectly enjoyable, and ideal for everyday drinking. Some wines, however, are really special, and here we look at how wine enthusiasts identify these. We also look at how to recognise if a wine is damaged or faulty.

VINE HEALTH *There are various diseases that can affect the vine and the grape, but wine producers are wise to the signs of disease, so that unhealthy grapes never make it to your glass.*

WHAT IS GOOD WINE?

Let's start by defining what is meant by good and bad quality wine in the most general sense. The first point to consider is that taste is always subjective. The professionals define a good wine as having the following characteristics:

- It has balanced flavour and texture.
- It has good length (the flavour lingers in your mouth).
- It has complexity (it reveals many flavours).

WHAT IS BAD WINE?

A "bad" wine usually refers to a wine that has been damaged, is faulty or has been manufactured poorly. Happily, production methods and shop buying policies have improved so much in recent years that you will rarely encounter a bad wine. If you encounter a wine that has a fault, it is usually as a result of poor bottling or imperfect storage conditions.

Recognizing a damaged or faulty bottle can be difficult, especially if you are unfamiliar with the wine. You need to look at, smell and taste the wine to assess it fully. We look at the etiquette of tasting wine in a restaurant in detail on pages 142–3.

Corked wine

This is the most common fault, and is caused by a fungus-affected cork coming into contact with the wine at the bottling stage of the winemaking process. The fungus, called TCA (2,4,6–Trichloroanisole), causes the wine to take on a musty aroma – the smell is very similar to that of damp or wet cardboard. In this case, the affected wine can be said to be "corked" or to have "cork taint". Bad cases of cork taint are obvious, but experts can disagree about mild cases. The term

"corked wine" is often misused and does not refer to wine that contains pieces of cork (see page 121).

Discoloured wine

If a wine looks brown, has lost its aroma and tastes flat or of cooked fruit, the most likely cause is excessive exposure to oxygen. This happens if the wine has been stored incorrectly, or if the wine has been opened and left for a few days.

Vinegar-flavoured wine

If a wine tastes of vinegar or tastes sour, it has been damaged by bacterial infection. Some wines are naturally high in acidity, but they will taste very different from a wine that has turned to vinegar.

Mould on the cork

An old wine, which has been stored for some time, may have mould growing on the outside end of the cork. This is not necessarily a bad sign; it may mean that the wine has simply been stored in humid conditions. It is unlikely that the wine inside the bottle will be affected.

Crystals in the wine

If your wine has small white crystals in the bottom of the glass or bottle, they are not pieces of glass, but tartaric crystals. These result from the precipitation of tartaric acid contained in wine and are perfectly harmless. You can decant the wine to get rid of them, if you like, but if you don't, the wine will still be perfectly drinkable.

IDENTIFYING FAULTS *Some of the worst faults are only evident when you smell and/or taste the wine. Some of the faults we see are not faults at all, and when removed, leave the wine perfectly drinkable. Pieces of cork in the wine (top), a damaged cork (middle) and crystal deposits (bottom) are not signs of faulty wine.*

sommelier savoir faire

■ It is very common for pieces of cork to crumble when the cork is removed, particularly in an old bottle of wine. They do not mean that the wine is faulty, and will not affect the flavour of the wine. At home, simply remove them from your glass. In a restaurant, ask the sommelier to remove them. He or she will remove the bottle, decant the wine, and return it to the table in the decanter.

■ If you have opened wine at home that you suspect is faulty, re-cork it and take it back to the store the following day, ideally with the receipt. If you are in doubt, pour a glass and leave it for 1–2 hours, keeping the bottle uncorked. If the wine is faulty, the fault will be more evident when you return to it.

 *Wine with*

GAME

It is the process of hanging game meat for several days that gives it its richness and potent flavour. If serving game for a special meal, you'll need a good-quality full-bodied red wine to complement the luxurious nature of the meat and to suit the occasion.

Pigeon

You'll need quite a powerful and mature red to cope with the richness and high fat content of roast pigeon.

Côte de Nuits *A full-bodied Burgundy with maturity and a powerful flavour.*

Tuscan Sangiovese *This is robust enough to cope with the distinctive taste of pigeon and works well with plain vegetable side dishes.*

Pheasant

Whether the pheasant is from the wild, or has been farmed, it is best served with a fine, mature red Bordeaux.

Pomerol *The richness of this Bordeaux will complement the richness and texture of the meat.*

St Emilion *Go for a fine quality aged bottle that will really do justice to your meal. Add a splash of St Emilion to the cooking juices for a delicious sauce.*

Quail

Not as rich as most other game birds, quails are delicious grilled or barbecued. Choose a light red to accompany quail.

Young Burgundy *Choose one that is soft and fresh enough not to drown the delicate flavours of the quail.*

Pinot Noir *One from the New World would be a good option.*

Rioja *The flavours of a mature Rioja will complement quail beautifully.*

Rabbit

For stew, the rabbit is usually marinaded in a rich red wine for several hours before cooking, so you'll require a well-matched red for drinking. Go for big flavours.

Bordeaux *Choose one of the more youthful red Bordeaux.*

Côtes de Frontonnais *This is a more savoury red, ideal for rabbit served roasted.*

Chinon *This medium-bodied red with good fruit and acidity will also marry well with a fruity sauce.*

Hare

The flavour of hare is stronger than rabbit; the meat is darker in colour, and the overriding flavour is "gamier". Accordingly, you should serve a full-bodied red.

Nuits-St-Georges *The sturdiness of this wine will withstand the strong game flavour.*

Ribera del Duero *A luxurious, big Spanish red.*

Barbaresco *Very powerful, full-flavoured and aromatic.*

Venison

Lean cuts of venison can dry out during cooking, so serve medium-rare with a sauce made from the cooking juices. Forequarter cuts should be marinaded in wine before cooking to tenderise the meat.

Syrah *This is rich and gamey enough to take on the distinctive flavour of venison.*

Chianti *A 3–4 year old Chianti will have a similar mouthfeel to a softly cooked tender fillet.*

CASSEROLED RABBIT WITH SEASONAL VEGETABLES Serve with a Chinon or a red Bordeaux.

RECOGNIZING *Grape* VARIETIES

There are thousands of grape varieties in the world, and most are capable of producing good wine. The most popular and widely available wines are made from about fifty grape varieties, and they can taste very different depending on where in the world they are grown. Learning to recognize their key characteristics can take a lifetime of tasting.

KEY FLAVOURS

The flavours we associate with red grapes (sometimes called black grapes) tend to be those of red and black soft fruits. We tend to associate the flavours of white grape wines with citrus or stone fruits, perhaps with hints of oak and toast. Climate plays a key role in determining the flavour of a particular wine, and you will find variations between wines produced in different countries, regions and at different times of the year. On pages 86–7 and pages 88–9, we outline the key characteristics of the major red and white grapes to help you to identify them in a blind tasting, or identify the ones you particularly enjoy.

Tannin and oak

The one thing you shouldn't expect to find in white wine that you do in red is tannin. Tannin is the flavour and texture that comes from grape skins and pips, and white wines are fermented without these. Tannin levels vary in red wines, according to the grape variety and how the wine is made.

The taste of oak is found in both white and red wines. Chardonnay, Semillon and Sauvignon Blanc may be aged in new oak, and have an affinity with the flavour. Riesling and Gewürztraminer are better without a flavour of new oak.

VARIETIES AND VARIETALS

Most New World wine producers label their wines according to the grape variety, whereas the leading European producers label them according to where they came from, namely, the region, property and/or vineyard. The Appellation Contrôlée system usually forbids French wine producers from putting the grape variety on the label. This may lead to confusion for someone discussing a wine or reading a label. To summarize, the term "variety" refers to the different grapes and their characteristics; the term "varietal" refers to a wine made almost entirely of one grape (at least 85 per cent), as opposed to a blended wine.

BLENDING

Many winemakers blend wines, whether from the same or different grape varieties. It is not unusual for winemakers to blend different vintages to ensure consistency of a particular style of wine, and some do it to keep the cost down. For example, in the USA, Chardonnay and Colombard wines are often blended to reduce the cost of expensive Chardonnay.

Not all red grapes blend happily with each other, but some blend to such good effect that a blend is better than each grape on its own. Red Bordeaux is a blend of cabernet sauvignon, cabernet franc and merlot – all these grapes are good on their own, but more often than not, they're better together. Champagne and Châteauneuf-du-Pape are also blended wines.

Cabernet sauvignon is a useful blending partner with many different grapes, though if handled carelessly it can dominate too much. It's particularly good with shiraz in Australia and sangiovese in Italy. Tempranillo and garnacha are often found together in Spain, and the blend of grenache, mourvèdre and syrah is typical of southern France.

IN WITH THE NEW The Don Maximiano estate in Chile was one of the first New World vineyards to grow the French cabernet sauvignon grape.

grape varieties

The most common grape varieties are discussed in detail on the following pages, but here are some others that you are likely to encounter in your wine tasting:

Barbera Originally from north-west Italy. Grown successfully in California. High tannin, bitter cherry fruit, plum and cherry flavour. High acidity.

Cabernet franc From Bordeaux. Mostly grown as a blending grape to go with cabernet sauvignon and merlot. Light redcurrant fruit, quite grassy.

Carmenère Found in Chile, where growers planted it under the impression that it was merlot. Big, rich, plummy fruit, some spice. Low acidity.

Dolcetto A grape of north-west Italy, and the one the locals drink young and fresh. Bitter chocolate and cherry fruit.

Gamay The grape behind Beaujolais: it is not the same grape as the one Californians call gamay beaujolais. Light bubblegum and strawberry fruit, low tannin.

Grenache/garnacha A grape grown all over southern France and Spain, and now in California too. Rich, soft, toffee, plum and butter.

Malbec Grown in Argentina, it originated in Bordeaux, where it is now hardly grown. Rich redcurrant fruit. High acidity.

Mourvèdre Southern French grape of high quality. Also found in some Californian blends. High tannin, powerful, herby fruit. High acidity.

Pinotage South Africa's speciality. A flavour of redcurrant fruit and some spice.

Pinot blanc Loosely related to chardonnay – nut, apple or peach, but always much quieter and more neutral than chardonnay.

Pinot gris Spicy, dry to sweet wines. Alsace versions are rich and full; as pinot grigio in Italy it makes light, crisp wines.

Viognier Aromatic, apricot-flavoured grape found in the Rhône and the south of France – and increasingly elsewhere.

*CABERNET SAUVIGNON
The most famous red wine
grape, this is one of the
main Bordeaux grapes (the
others are merlot and
cabernet franc). It has
spread to almost every
wine-making country.*

*MERLOT A traditional
blending partner for
cabernet sauvignon, this is
also extremely popular on
its own.*

On the nose Characteristically,
blackcurrant, plums, perhaps
vanilla if the wine has been aged
in new oak. Some have a smell of
mint. Less ripe versions may have
a note of green capsicums.

On the palate Plum and
blackcurrant. Good tannic
structure. Many Cabernet
Sauvignons have an addition of
merlot.

On the nose Plum, cherry, even
strawberry and raspberry.

On the palate Softer, fleshier
and lower in acidity, merlot can
lack cabernet sauvignon's tannic
backbone, which is why they are
so good blended together.

*NEBBIOLO The great red
grape of Piedmont, in
north-west Italy. Grown
elsewhere with mixed
results.*

*PINOT NOIR A seductive
grape, making silky reds. It's
the only grape used for red
Burgundy; there are also
good examples in New
Zealand, Oregon and
California. A classic
sparkling wine grape.*

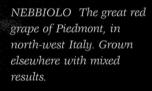

On the nose Typically, tar and
rose. This is a wine that is both
big and aromatic. Look also for
chocolate, coffee and herbs.

On the palate Rich, weighty,
and flavoursome. Expect high
tannins, plus chocolate, tar and
rose. High acidity.

On the nose Strawberry, cherry,
violet, forest undergrowth and
perhaps a touch of cabbage.

On the palate Good acidity,
relatively low tannin; strawberry,
undergrowth, vegetables, game,
plus a silky texture.

SANGIOVESE An Italian grape that has spread further than nebbiolo. It is the main grape behind Chianti and is widely grown in central and southern Italy. Also grown successfully in Australia and California.

On the nose Tobacco, raisin, coffee, cherry, tea.

On the palate High tannin, plus bitter cherry, coffee, tobacco, perhaps raisin and a bitter twist at the end. High acidity.

SYRAH The fine red grape of the northern Rhône Valley in France has also made a home in Australia, where it is known as shiraz. Known as either syrah or shiraz in California.

On the nose Smoke, herbs, liquorice, blackcurrant, loganberry, leather. Rhône examples tend to be more smoke and herbs; Australian ones are more blackcurrant and leather.

On the palate High tannin, very rich fruit. An intense flavour – smoke and herbs. Australian ones are broad, fat, fruity; Rhône ones are tannic, herby. High acidity.

ZINFANDEL California's specialty, made in every possible style, from sweetish "blush" wines to red blockbusters.

On the nose Plum, blackberry, spice, earth. Lighter ones are more cherry and redcurrant. Blush Zinfandels are mildly strawberry smelling.

On the palate Big, rich wine full of tannin. Spice and blackberry. Lighter ones have less tannin and less assertive structure; blush ones are sweeter. High acidity.

TEMPRANILLO One of Spain's principal red grapes, it's the basis of most Rioja.

On the nose Strawberry, vanilla, toffee.

On the palate Can be quite light with a vanilla–strawberry taste, or big, rich, lush and quite tannic.

CHARDONNAY The most famous white grape, which has spread from Burgundy in France to all over the world. It's an excellent traveller and styles vary according to climate.

On the nose Often influenced or even dominated by the vanilla smell of new oak. Also nuts, butter, cream, toast, biscuits, melon, mango, pineapple.

On the palate Firm structure in cool climates, softer in warm climates. Butter, cream, toast, tropical fruits. Medium acidity.

CHENIN BLANC In France's Loire Valley, this grape makes top-class wines that range from very dry to very sweet. Examples from elsewhere (such as South Africa) are usually dull.

On the nose Apple, lemon, honey, a mineral streak.

On the palate Dry ones are minerally, all apples and lemons, austere in youth but honeyed after a few years; sweet ones are honeyed, all apricots and peaches. High acidity, whether sweet or dry.

GEWÜRZTRAMINER Exotically perfumed – especially in Alsace, its homeland. Other regions (Germany, Austria, New Zealand, Washington State, Oregon) make more restrained versions.

On the nose Lychee, sweet spice, rose, face cream.

On the palate All the above, plus a touch of pepper and coffee. Low acidity.

MUSCAT The one grape variety whose wine tastes of grapes. Muscat blanc à petits grains is the most elegant. Muscat grapes are used to make both dry and sweet wines, as well as sparkling.

On the nose Freshly picked grapes. Roses, orange peel, apple and raisin on dark, sweet wines.

On the palate Almost crunchily fresh grapes, apple and orange. Sweet ones – raisin, intense. Low acidity.

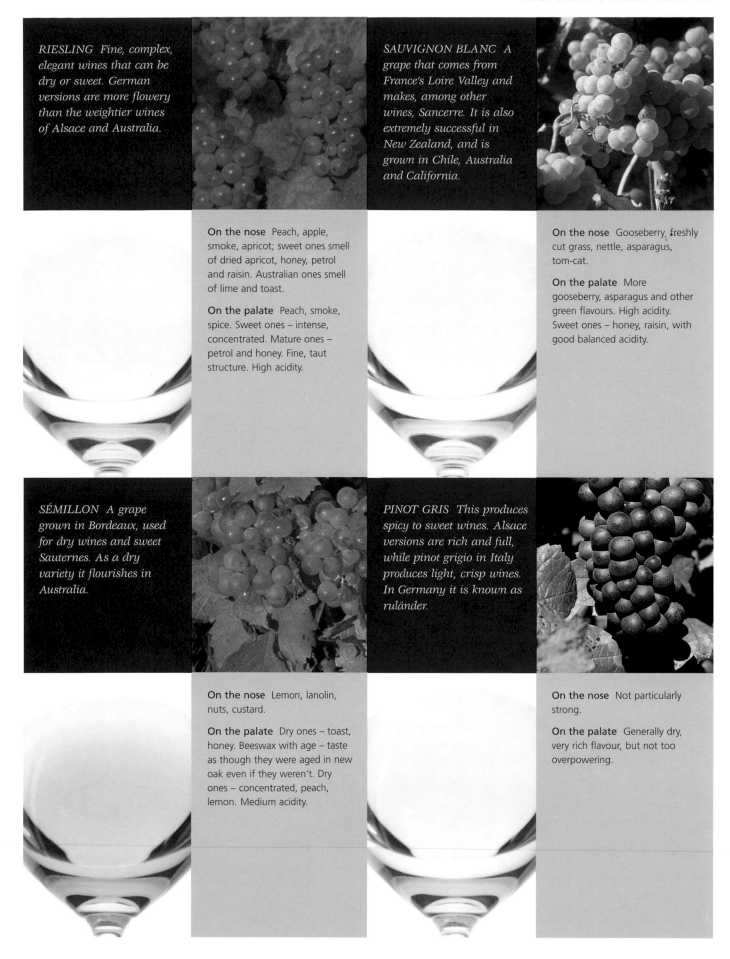

RIESLING *Fine, complex, elegant wines that can be dry or sweet. German versions are more flowery than the weightier wines of Alsace and Australia.*

On the nose Peach, apple, smoke, apricot; sweet ones smell of dried apricot, honey, petrol and raisin. Australian ones smell of lime and toast.

On the palate Peach, smoke, spice. Sweet ones – intense, concentrated. Mature ones – petrol and honey. Fine, taut structure. High acidity.

SAUVIGNON BLANC *A grape that comes from France's Loire Valley and makes, among other wines, Sancerre. It is also extremely successful in New Zealand, and is grown in Chile, Australia and California.*

On the nose Gooseberry, freshly cut grass, nettle, asparagus, tom-cat.

On the palate More gooseberry, asparagus and other green flavours. High acidity. Sweet ones – honey, raisin, with good balanced acidity.

SÉMILLON *A grape grown in Bordeaux, used for dry wines and sweet Sauternes. As a dry variety it flourishes in Australia.*

On the nose Lemon, lanolin, nuts, custard.

On the palate Dry ones – toast, honey. Beeswax with age – taste as though they were aged in new oak even if they weren't. Dry ones – concentrated, peach, lemon. Medium acidity.

PINOT GRIS *This produces spicy to sweet wines. Alsace versions are rich and full, while pinot grigio in Italy produces light, crisp wines. In Germany it is known as ruländer.*

On the nose Not particularly strong.

On the palate Generally dry, very rich flavour, but not too overpowering.

POULTRY

There is an assumption that white meat should be served with white wine, but this isn't necessarily the case. Each type of poultry has a distinctive flavour of its own and your choice of wine should reflect the cooking method and the ingredients with which it is prepared and served.

Chicken

Roast chicken can taste quite different to a grilled, baked or poached bird, and a great deal of flavour can result from the type of sauce that you use and even the components of the stuffing or accompaniment that you use.

Also, meat from two different parts of the bird can be contrasting in flavour – the meat from the thigh is darker and more flavoursome than breast meat. You'll need to consider all of these factors when you are looking for a wine to match your chicken-based meal.

Chablis *This crisp and lively wine will complement the perennial favourite roast chicken.*
Riesling *For a skinless poached breast, choose a lighter-bodied white.*
Sancerre *Served on its own, the darker thigh meat requires a strong wine with a little age.*
Shiraz *You could choose a young red for roast or grilled chicken.*
Gewürztraminer *This will cope with the fragrance and flavour of a spiced dish, such as a Thai curry.*

Goose

Fatty and rich, goose is often served with fruit sauce to balance the high fat content. It is also often served with foie gras. Choose an opulent and acidic red wine with a fruit flavour to cut through the richness.

Shiraz *One from Australia's Clare Valley has good fruit and acidity.*
Cahors *These are notable for their good colour and full body, and taste delicious with roast goose.*

Duck

This is another rich and succulent bird, with its own distinctive flavour. Add a fruit-based sauce such as cherry or orange, and you have a delicious complex dish that needs a gutsy wine.

Red Rhône *Choose an older Rhône with some fruit character.*
Red Burgundy *For duck with a mushroom-based sauce, you'll need a less fruity wine.*

Guinea fowl

A bit of a delicacy, guinea fowl are often roasted with strips of bacon laid over the top or marinaded to prevent the meat from drying out.

Pinot Noir *A quality red such as Volnay will work well with the rich flavour of the bird.*
White Burgundy *Go for a mature bottle for the best balance.*
Red Rhône *Choose a young red Rhône for a soft flavour.*

Turkey

This is richer-tasting than chicken and so requires a fuller-bodied wine to pick up its flavours. Serve with something special at Christmas.

Zinfandel *Roast turkey served with cranberry sauce would suit a wine with fruitiness and body.*
Shiraz *This has the ripeness and full body to cope with roast turkey and all the trimmings.*

ROAST TURKEY WITH CRANBERRY SAUCE Serve a special Shiraz or Zinfandel with a traditional Christmas meal.

ATTENDING A *Tasting*

There are several kinds of wine tasting, but most are held to encourage or enable you to buy wine. Wine tasting holidays and courses are arranged for enjoyment, and will be hosted by individuals who will guide you through the tasting process. Here we explain how to taste wine for possible purchase.

TASTING OPPORTUNITIES

Attending tastings is a great way to experience a variety of wines without having to purchase them. If you choose to buy a bottle, you can be sure that you will like it – which makes far more sense than risking an untried purchase.

If you're touring a vineyard or winery, you'll usually be offered a glass or two of wine at the end of the tour. Other tastings are held by wine merchants or retailers, and they can take either an informal approach – opening one or two bottles for keen customers – or they may be more formal events, perhaps held out of normal working hours, or as a sales promotion for a particular wine.

If you are planning to place a large order, it is reasonable to ask to taste the wine before you buy, although many retailers will open a bottle for you only if the order is for expensive wine, in large quantities. If you want to buy several cases of an inexpensive wine, the retailer might suggest that you buy a single bottle to take home to taste.

If you're not used to such events, a tasting can confuse your palate so that you think you like – or dislike – a wine more than you really do. Taking a bottle home, and tasting it at your leisure, can be the best way to decide if you really like a wine.

Informal shop tasting

A shop will often have one or two bottles open for customers to sample, to encourage you to taste something new, or to promote a particular wine. Take the glass or sample on offer, or ask the person in charge of pouring to give you a taste. You probably won't be offered more than a third of a glass of each

STAY FOCUSED Take your time over each wine in a tasting and concentrate on everything that you experience, so that you can get the most out of each wine.

wine. Feel free to ask questions. The staff should be happy to give you information about the grape variety, country and producer of the wine. You'll find that you are welcome to taste everything that's open. As you will be sampling only small amounts, there is no need to spit out the wine. If crackers are supplied, eat between tasting each wine to cleanse the palate, or you could ask for a glass of water.

Formal merchant's or shop tasting

Some merchants hold invitation-only tastings for regular customers or people who have expressed interest in buying a large quantity of wine. There could be a large selection of wines open, so you need to take a focused approach. Decide what to try before you begin, and limit yourself to no more than a dozen wines. You could choose to taste only white wines, or a particular grape variety, such as Chardonnay or Zinfandel. A focused tasting can be an excellent way of building your knowledge of wine. You can learn from your fellow tasters, too – people are bound to discuss the wines as they sample them, so even if you don't feel confident enough to voice your opinion, listen out for what the other tasters say.

Servers will pour the samples for you so that the merchant can control the quantity of wine consumed. As with an informal tasting, expect to get no more than a third of a glass each time. You will probably be expected to use the same glass for each wine. Whether you swallow or spit out the wine is up to you: spittoons will almost certainly be provided, and many tasters will use them. If you decide to swallow, however, limit the number of wines you taste – otherwise you will find it increasingly difficult to taste the wines accurately. Mineral water and dry crackers are usually provided and can help to refresh your palate between wines. Cheese may be offered also, but the strong flavour can confuse your palate, so it is best avoided for the most accurate tasting.

how to spit

Everybody who has brushed their teeth knows how to spit; the knack at a wine tasting is to do it carefully and with confidence in public. Practise at home if you feel shy. A professional spittoon is a metal funnel about 1 m (3 ft) high, but a spittoon can take many forms, including containers placed on a counter, or a bucket on the floor. Try to be accurate, and not to splash yourself or other people – there may be other tasters close by, awaiting their turn. After spitting, move away from the spittoon to give the next taster adequate space.

Vineyard or winery tasting

After a tour of the vineyard, a wine producer will usually offer a few wines for tasting. You will probably be offered only a small selection of wine, and rarely the vineyard's most expensive wines. If there are other bottles already open you can ask to taste those as well, but don't ask for bottles that are not open unless you are a serious buyer. Some vineyards charge a nominal fee, which they can refund if you make a large purchase. Spittoons are usually provided, but if not, it's usual practice to ask for one or to go outside and spit on the gravel or grass.

Tasting etiquette

Order of tasting Whatever the tasting occasion, a general rule is to taste white wines before red, and light wines before heavier wines, to allow your palate to adjust. A host may suggest a tasting order. If you are tasting several vintages of the same wine (a vertical tasting), taste the youngest wines first. A tasting may focus on one region or grape variety, so the order of tasting will be less important. Ask your host if you are unsure about the tasting order.

What to wear Unless a dress code is stipulated, there is no need to dress formally. At evening tastings held by merchants for their customers, most people will arrive straight from work, and will be dressed accordingly. Visiting vineyards or wineries is generally a weekend or holiday occupation, and nobody minds what you wear. Dark colours can be more prudent, because wine spills easily. Most white wine won't stain, but red will (see page 125).

What not to wear Strong perfume or aftershave can interfere with accurate tasting, so go au naturel – even if you don't notice the scent, the other tasters will. The smell of tobacco smoke can also be distracting, so refrain from smoking during a tasting.

What to take If you want to make a note of the wines and write down what you think of them, you may wish to take a notebook and a pen. Note the information on the label, along with your tasting notes (see opposite) to enable you later to identify the wines you enjoyed.

To buy or not to buy Don't feel pressurised to buy wine that isn't to your taste, or fails to meet your requirements. Use your judgement: if you've had a personal tour of a vineyard with the owner who has opened bottles for you especially, buying a couple of bottles as a thankyou is appropriate. Large tourist-orientated vineyards do not expect all visitors to buy, but you may find that buying direct from the producer may afford good value. At a merchant's or shop tasting, equally, there's no need to buy – you may prefer to consider your choices and revisit later.

A VINEYARD TASTING
Visiting a vineyard is one of the best ways to try a range of wines. You can just turn up to the larger wineries, but you will need to make an appointment with small, specialist wineries. Several travel companies arrange tours, which can be a great way to meet fellow wine enthusiasts.

Assessing Wines

The problem with tasting more than two or three wines together is remembering what you've tasted – your nose and palate can get confused. You need to develop a taste memory so you can differentiate between wines.

TASTE AND MEMORY

In some ways, training your palate is easier than training your memory – learning to taste wine means utilizing sensory abilities that nature provided you with at birth – it's just a question of practice.

You need to form your own associations that will remind you of wine flavours. On pages 86–9 we give lists of grape varieties and their common associated flavours, and on page 77 we look at other widely used tasting terms and what they generally mean – these can be a useful starting point.

When you next try a wine, take a look at the list of associated flavours. Look for them in the wine, but don't pretend you find them if you don't – few wines contain all the possible flavours for that grape variety. Try to think of specific flavours – "fruity" and "tangy" are not specific enough to stay in your mind and help you distinguish between wines. But if you tell yourself, "gooseberries" or "apples", you will remember more.

Check-list

If you're stuck for what to say about a wine, it may help you to run these ideas through your mind.

- *Does it smell of: oak, nuts, spice, fruit? If fruit, what sort?*
- *Does it taste: tannic, acidic, soft, rich, lean, oaky?*
- *Does it taste balanced? If not, why not?*
- *Is the finish long or short?*

WRITE IT DOWN

The best way to remember what you've decided about a wine is to write it down. It is particularly important to have a record of which ones you liked, and why, if you want to compare notes with someone else, or if you are planning to make a purchase at the end of the tasting.

You could start by writing down "colour", "aroma" and "taste", and write your thoughts alongside these headings. You may look at the colour of a wine and note: Deep red, almost black – not much sign of ageing. As you nose it: Very spicy. Minerals. Good fruit – blackberries. After tasting you might put: Soft tannins. Still quite young. Nice balance, long finish.

TASTING NOTES Your tasting notes don't have to be highly detailed, and you will develop your own personal system. A good aide-mémoire is to work through a tasting checklist of colour, aroma and taste.

GRADING WINE

Most leading wine critics adopt a numerical assessment system – it's particularly helpful for readers, and can be very useful for the private enthusiast who wants to catalogue tastings over the years.

The famous American wine critic, Robert Parker, devised a system of marking wines based on the American high school grading system. You mark out of 100, where 50 is the base. According to Parker's system:

50–69 is below average to poor.

70–79 is average.

80–89 is above average to very good.

90–95 is outstanding.

96–100 is extraordinary.

Other systems work on points out of 20, where 10 is the pass mark for an average wine. Obviously, the larger the scale, the more flexibility you'll have.

VEGETARIAN DISHES

There are so many possibilities in the vegetarian diet that there is no need to miss out on the more robust red wines, just because your diet is meat-free. Here are suggestions for wines to go with some of the vegetarian staples. See pages 104–5 for wines to go with spicy foods.

Pasta

Pasta in itself is neutral in taste; it is the sauce that will dictate the type of wine you will need as an accompaniment.

Chardonnay Choose an unoaked style to go with vegetable-based pasta dishes.
Swiss Chasselas With a creamy sauce, you'll need a dry white with medium body.
Chianti Serve a robust red with baked pasta dishes such as lasagne.

Rice

A vegetable risotto needs a wine that will complement its creamy consistency and the flavour of its ingredients and will not drown it with too much flavour.

Pinot Grigio Light, crisp and delicate enough for a simple risotto.
Pinot Blanc This is fragrant and crisp with a slight apple acidity that will bring contrast to a rice-based meal.

Vegetables

For a simple dish of roast Mediterranean vegetables, such as aubergine, courgette, tomato and pepper, look for a wine with a hint of acidity.

Merlot An Italian Merlot has the full body and slight acidity to handle a range of vegetables.
Rosé The Italian rosé Lagrein-Kretzer is ideal for baked vegetable dishes, because it is soft and well-balanced with a hint of bitterness. A French rosé would also be a good choice.

Eggs

Flans, quiches, tortillas and other egg-based dishes require a wine that goes with their creamy textures and the flavour of any other ingredients.

Chardonnay For egg and cheese dishes, choose an unoaked style.
Pinot Gris If there are onions in the dish, go for one of the drier styles.
Sauvignon Blanc This youthful and fruity wine will cut through the creamy texture of most egg dishes.

Cheese dishes

Some cheeses don't work well with wine (see pages 116–7), but cooked cheese dishes, such as bakes, aren't usually a problem. Choose a wine that will lift the meal without introducing too strong a flavour.

Semillon-Chardonnay The Australian style is perfect with most baked cheese dishes.
Sauvignon Blanc With a rich fondue, try those from the New World.

Nuts and beans

For a nut-based salad such as a Waldorf, you'll need a light, flavoursome wine that will work with strong flavours and textures, but also will be refreshing. Roast nut or bean dishes will need a robust red wine.

Italian Moscato With a little acid, notes of nuttiness and apple overtones, this is ideal for salads.
Chilean Merlot For a nut roast, a medium- or full- bodied red is perfect.

VEGETABLE SPRING ROLLS Serve with a fresh, lively rosé.

Blind Tasting

Taking a glass of wine with no clues as to what it might be and guessing the grape variety, region and year from the colour, nose and palate alone is a particular skill – it requires a very well-honed taste memory. It is an enjoyable and rewarding skill to learn, however, so why not give it a go? You can blind taste for fun with a group of like-minded friends or you can really test yourself and use it as serious practice for professional blind tasting examinations.

BLIND JUSTICE

Tasting a wine without knowing anything about it is an extremely good way of testing your prejudices. You may think you dislike a particular grape variety, but you might not even spot it in a blind tasting; or you may consider a certain wine to be of extremely high or low quality, but do you have the same opinion when you don't know how much it cost?

WHERE DO YOU START?

A blind tasting can be a little bit daunting – you could be faced with perhaps 20 glasses of wine, all almost the same colour. You should be given a sheet of paper with space for you to note down the grape variety, the country and region of origin and the vintage of each wine. You might also be invited to comment on the quality of the wine and perhaps give it a mark (see page 95). Don't feel overwhelmed – all you need to do is to take your time with each wine and ask yourself a series of questions that progressively narrow the field of choice (see opposite). Aim for a definitive conclusion, but if you cannot decide which wine it is, detailed tasting notes will allow you to participate in discussion.

Practice makes perfect
If you're an inexperienced taster, there are probably some grape varieties and wine styles with which you are still unfamiliar. These are potential traps in a blind tasting – you might taste something unfamiliar and mark it down because you think it's a strange example of something you know well. There's no way to avoid this – even experienced tasters get things wrong.

An eminent wine critic was once asked if he'd ever mistaken Bordeaux for Burgundy. "Not since luncheon", was his reply. Try to take mistakes in good humour, as they are an important part of the learning process.

The key questions

Appearance How does it look: is it clear or dull, pale or deep? What is its colour: lemon or gold, pink or orange, purple, ruby or tawny?

A dark colour in a white wine can indicate a warm climate or is sometimes a sign of greater maturity.

Nose How does it smell: clean, weak or pronounced; fruity, floral, vegetal or spicy?

Rich, tropical fruit flavours in a white wine and hot, spicy, slightly jammy characters in a red are clues to a warm climate. Conversely, steely acidity in a white will make you think of cool climates, as will elegance in a red. The nose is probably your greatest clue to the grape variety.

Palate How does it taste: is it sweet or acidic, fruity, floral, vegetal or spicy? Is it tannic? How does it feel on your palate: is it full-bodied, and does it linger in your mouth?

Run through your mental check-list of grape flavours and see which apply. Feel the structure of the wine as well – that will give you just as many clues. For example, if it's white and smells and tastes of ripe apricots but has low acidity, it is more likely to be Chardonnay than Riesling, since Riesling is acidic.

Quality Does the wine have good length? Does it linger in the memory? Is it poor, acceptable or good? Do you think it will improve with further age; is it at its peak now; or even past its best?

This check-list is based upon the Wine and Spirit Education Trust (WSET) guidelines for making tasting notes.

GETTING TO KNOW GRAPES Recognizing the key characteristics of the main grape varieties is invaluable for accurate blind tasting (see pages 84–9).

PLAYING WITH OPTIONS

One way in which novice tasters can build up confidence in their skills while having a bit of fun is to play the options game – devised by Australian wine connoisseur Len Evans. You'll need a few fellow tasters and a question-master who knows his or her wines. The question-master will give you a series of options to help you to narrow down the identity of the wine you are blind tasting. You may be given three possible countries, followed by three regions; three vineyards; a choice of vintages. Players remain in the game only by consistently choosing correctly.

Narrowing your choices

If you know that the wine you are tasting is one type – for example, a Sauvignon Blanc – but that is all you know, ask yourself these questions to lead you to a specific wine:

■ Is it from a cool or a warm climate?
Gooseberry favours – cool climate.
Melon and peach – warm climate.

■ If cool, is it European or New World?
New World examples may have more up-front fruit; European ones may taste more minerally.

■ If European, is it French?
France is the main source of the sauvignon blanc grape in Europe, but it is grown in Austria, Spain and Italy, too.

■ If French, is it from Bordeaux, the Loire or the South?
Probably not the South, if you've decided it's cool climate.

■ Is it a young wine or an old wine?
Bear in mind that Loire Sauvignon Blanc matures quickly.

■ If young, how young? A year old? Two years?
An extra year will make it taste quite a bit rounder.

Planning a Wine Tasting

Opening and comparing a range of bottles and discussing their characteristics is a good way of placing wine in context and identifying which wines you enjoy most. You, could, of course, plan a comparative tasting just for yourself, but it can be more interesting to have other people there, particularly to discuss ideas and perhaps to share costs. Wine drinking doesn't have to be a serious business, but you will get more out of your glass of wine if you know what to look for.

Ideal conditions

Forward planning is the key to a successful wine tasting. Ideally, hold your tasting in the morning or, if the thought of alcohol that early is too much, arrange it for early evening or before dinner. A meal will deaden your palate, while hunger will sharpen it.

Some people like to taste in silence, so that they can concentrate on their taste sensations undistracted by other people's comments. Others like to discuss the wines as they go, to share impressions and ideas. Decide with your group in advance, and let all guests know the group rules.

Think about where you want to hold the tasting. You could hire a location if you are nervous about spills or don't have enough space. If you want to hold it at home, consider the following:

- *Choose a room large enough for a table with space for guests to move around freely. Where will you put used glasses and something to spit into?*
- *Does the room have good natural light? Place the glasses of wine on a white tablecloth and in adequate light, so that guests can see the colour properly.*
- *Make sure there are no distracting smells in the room, such as strongly scented flowers, room fragrance or food. Ask your guests in advance not to wear perfume or aftershave, which can also compete with the aroma of the wine.*

TASTING GLASSES If you want to invest in specialist tasting glasses, choose an ISO (International Standards Organisation) glass, or one like this from Riedel where you fill the stem with wine, and roll the glass to release the aroma.

Choose a theme

A themed tasting is often more interesting than a random tasting, and can be a good way to distinguish the subtle differences between wines. You could choose wines from the same region or the same grape variety.

Ask each taster to bring a bottle – you may want to suggest a price range – and each person could bring information about the wine that relates to the theme. The most widely used themes are:

Vertical tasting A comparison of different vintages of the same wine.

Horizontal tasting A comparison of different wines of the same vintage.

Comparative tasting A comparison of different examples of the same style of wine.

Blind tasting Identifying an unmarked wine.

Putting the wines in order

At a themed tasting, one of the most popular ways of putting the wines in order is according to price, with the cheapest wine first. You could also try serving them in order of heaviness, with the lightest wine being tasted first, although you may not know how light or heavy each wine is until you've tasted it. The usual order for tasting wine is:

- *White before red.*
- *Young before old.*
- *Light before heavy.*
- *Dry before sweet.*

After the tasting, it can be nice to reward tasters for their efforts with a glass of something special. Choose a very different type of wine from the ones you have been tasting, to refresh the palate.

Tasting equipment checklist

Allow at least two hours beforehand to set out everything before people arrive. You will need:

Wine Calculate how much wine you will need on the premise that a 75 cl bottle will hold approximately 15 tasting servings. If you want to monitor consumption, don't allow tasters to pour the wine themselves.

Corkscrew If you're opening a dozen bottles or more, you'll want an efficient corkscrew that is fast and needs little effort (see pages 119–20).

Plenty of clean glasses You'll need at least one glass per taster. A basic tulip-shaped glass (see page 130) will be fine. Many wine stores will hire glasses for a moderate charge, or may even lend them to you free of charge if you purchase a large quantity of wine. You can also buy specialist tasting glasses (see opposite).

Mineral water and biscuits To refresh your palate when needed, choose dry wafer biscuits – avoid salted or flavoured biscuits, which will affect the taste of the wine. Cheese is also too flavoursome to serve with wine for tasting.

Something to spit into A bucket is adequate, otherwise professional spittoons can be purchased from specialist suppliers. You could put

sawdust in the bottom, which absorbs the wine, and looks tidier, but is messy to dispose of afterwards.

Newspaper Collect plenty of paper to place under and around the bucket or spittoon, to protect the floor from wine. Few people, even professional tasters, are consistently accurate when spitting.

Clean linen cloth Useful for wiping drips from the neck of the bottle, if necessary. Have a roll of paper towels handy, as well, for spills.

Paper and pens You'll need enough for everyone to write their comments. You could compile a tasting sheet which lists the wines to be tasted, with space for comments and scores, if you choose.

Bottle covers If you want the tasting to be blind, you will need to cover the labels. This can be done with aluminium foil, bottle aprons or napkins. You will need labels, one per bottle, to number the bottles for easy reference for the tasters.

EDUCATING

Your Palate

When you have reached the stage where there are several wine types that you know you like, it can be tempting to stick with them because they're safe. Besides, experimenting can be an expensive and potentially disappointing process. Don't miss out, though – here are some ways to extend your choices, while limiting the risks.

TAKING THINGS FURTHER

The easiest way to start to broaden your tasting experience is to experiment with the wine on sale at your local shop. In the chart opposite we list some of the most popular wines and suggest wines that have similar characteristics. This will help to take some of the risk out of buying something new. If you want to experiment further, there are several options. You can attend organised tastings (see pages 92–3), take classes, go on wine holidays, or even start your own wine-tasting group. It could help to keep a log book to record your tasting notes. How you organise this will vary depending on what you want from your wine, but you could start with noting:

- The name of the wine.
- The name of the producer.
- The vintage.
- Where you bought/tasted it.
- How much it cost.

You could also score the wines (see page 95). This will help you get an accurate assessment of those wines you particularly enjoy – and those you don't.

Take a class

To find out what's available in your area, consult a local what's-on listing, or a national wine magazine like *Wine Spectator* or *Decanter* – the small ads in the back pages should reveal useful leads. You could also ask your wine merchant. Major wine auctioneers often offer excellent courses. There are also several good websites that list courses (see pages 186–7).

Try to get a feel for the level of the class – it may be a waste of time and money if they know less than you do. Likewise, you don't want to feel out of your depth.

If you want to study wine seriously, there are courses aimed at the wine trade that might appeal to you. Ask a good wine merchant to put you in touch with these, or contact the Wine and Spirit Educational Trust (see pages 186–7). Such courses are fairly expensive and require concentrated work. There may be an examination and a trade qualification attached.

Go on holiday

Wine holidays are organised by a number of specialist travel agents – look in the small ads in wine publications and websites (see pages 186–7), and travel websites for details. Find out who the tour leader is and how much wine experience he or she has. Ask how large the group usually is and the average level of knowledge. The brochure should give you a feel for how seriously a tour is taken by a winery – are there special tastings laid on, or just the standard winery tour?

Start a wine circle

If you have a number of like-minded friends, this can be a pleasant, informal way to expand your knowledge. Invite a small number of guests (no more than ten) to your home and ask them all to bring a bottle – it's a good idea to set price limits on the wines everybody brings, and to suggest a theme. For some tips on how to organise a wine-tasting evening, turn to pages 100–101. You should strike a happy balance between socialising and serious tasting to really learn something.

You could meet on a regular basis and take it in turns to act as host. If your friends are not keen, try placing a small ad in a wine or what's-on publication yourself. There may be lots of like-minded people in your area – you just haven't met them yet.

If you like

Red Burgundy
from France

Pinot Noir from California,
New Zealand or Chile

Rioja from Spain

Pinotage from South Africa

Shiraz
from Australia

Red Rhône from France

Blends of Syrah and
Grenache from California

Zinfandel from California

Toro and Ribera del Duero
from Spain

Red Douro from Portugal

Petite Sirah from Mexico

Merlot
from Chile

Pinotage from South Africa

Zinfandel from California

Merlot from California

Carmenère from Chile

Beaujolais from France

Reds from Valdepenas,
Navarra and La Mancha
in Spain

Cabernet Sauvignon
from California

Red Bordeaux from France

Cabernet Sauvignon from
Chile, New Zealand, Bulgaria
or South Africa

Zinfandel from California

Merlot from Chile

Pinotage from South Africa

If you like

Chardonnay
from California

Chardonnay
from Australia, Chile, Spain
or the South of France

Semillon from Australia

White Graves
from France

Mature white Rioja
from Spain

Sauvignon Blanc
from New Zealand

Sancerre from France

Pouilly-Fumé from France

Sauvignon Blanc from Chile
or Australia

Rueda from Spain

Riesling
from Germany

Riesling from Austria or
France

Scheurebe from Germany

Seyval Blanc from England

Semillon from Australia

Gewürztraminer
from Alsace, France

Gewürztraminer from Chile,
Washington State or Alto
Adige, Italy

Pinot Gris from Alsace,
France

Viognier from the Rhône,
France, or California

Dry Muscat from Alsace,
France or Australia

Wine with

SPICY FOODS

Some highly spiced foods can prove too much for a wine, but delicately spiced foods can be enhanced with a well-chosen wine. Serve a cooling salad or yogurt to calm the palate before drinking. Most spicy foods are best served with crisp, uplifting white wines, but there are exceptions.

Hot curries

Very spicy Indian curries can overwhelm the palate so serving with a fine wine is a waste – you simply won't be able to appreciate the subtle flavours. Wine is not part of the Indian culture and most would choose a yogurt drink or a beer. If you are drinking wine, make it crisp and light and serve chilled to take the edge off the heat.

Gewürztraminer This is probably the only wine that will taste good with a highly spiced curry.

Mild curries

Introducing yogurt to a curry or simply going easy on the spices produces a dish that is easier to match with wines.

Zinfandel The pepperiness of a white Zinfandel works well with most moderately spiced dishes.
Chardonnay Those from the New World are good with creamy curries such as korma.

Thai

Thai cuisine can be flavoured with chilli, lemon grass and other spices. You need to choose spicy white wines that can be served chilled.

Chablis This has the acidity and intensity to complement the spices. A Chablis Grand Cru, however, would have too much personality of its own to complement Thai cuisine.
Chardonnay Pick a New World wine to enhance nutty satay dishes.
Mosel This has a residual sugar that complements the intense spices.

Chinese

The tangy flavours in a Chinese meal are so finely tuned that you need a wine with subtlety.

Gewürztraminer A good choice to suit a Chinese meal, particularly the sweet and sour dishes.
Riesling With its delicate fruit flavors, acidity and sweetness, this works with most Chinese dishes.

Japanese

Although Japanese food is largely light and subtle, there is a tendency toward the odd sharp and vinegary mouthful. You need a wine strong enough to take on the sharpness, but light enough to match the delicacy of a Japanese meal.

Sake This traditional rice wine is the choice of most Japanese.
Beaujolais One of the few reds that works well with Japanese food.

Mexican

This cuisine does have a range of flavours and textures, but spicy tacos can be difficult to marry with wine. Nachos with sour cream and guacamole are easier to match.

Sangria Fruity and low in alcohol (see page 151), this is a good choice for all Mexican food.
Sauvignon Blanc The fruitiness will balance the spice – serve chilled to cleanse the palate.
Grenache You can drink red, but choose a lighter style.

STEAMED PRAWNS WITH THAI SPICES Serve with a chilled Chablis or Mosel.

ORDERING WINE IN A

Just as menus vary enormously, wine lists will vary according to the type of restaurant and how seriously it takes the wine it sells. The wide variety of wine lists, the range of information contained on them, and the tasting ritual all exist for the benefit of the consumer, so use them confidently and to your advantage.

NEGOTIATING A WINE LIST

Most wine lists are divided into sections. Some may simply separate red, white and sparkling; others may be organised by country and region. A third way is to list wines according to style, listing the light wines before the heavier ones. A helpful wine list will include the following information:

Item or bin number This can refer to where the wine is stored in the cellar, so do feel free to order wine according to its number. It will probably make life easier for the sommelier (French for wine waiter, pronounced *som-mel-yay*). Don't be surprised if, after ordering a wine by its name, the sommelier asks to see the list to take note of the number – it will be his reference in the cellar.

Name of the wine This can be the name of the grape, or the region. It can also refer to the name of the winery or producer. The identity of the producer is very important as it is the best guarantee of quality.

Vintage The year the wine was harvested.

Tasting notes These can be very useful when choosing which wine will suit your chosen meal. It usually helps to choose your food before you choose the wine.

Price Is the wine within your price range?

List design

Be a little wary of a huge list, bound in leather and looking as if it hasn't been updated for years. It can be very frustrating to read through a huge list, only to find the wine you would like is no longer available.

Some of the best wine lists are basic word-processed sheets that can be amended easily when the restaurant updates its stock of wine. The restaurant may even vary the list according to the season and to particular dishes on the menu.

Keep your options open

House wine These days, very few restaurants have poor house wines – the general standard of winemaking has improved such a lot. If a restaurant's wine list is good, the house wine should be good, too, and the proprietor will have selected it to complement the style of food and of cooking. Remember, the house wine is a restaurant's flagship – and therefore it should always be well-chosen, tasty and reliable.

Wine by the glass Ordering individual glasses of wine works out to be more expensive than a bottle. Before you order, think about how much wine you are going to drink. If you're likely to drink two glasses, it's more economical to buy a half-bottle; if you're likely to have four glasses, it's better to buy a bottle – even if you don't finish it. Some restaurants make a feature of wine by the glass, however, and have a wide selection. They may recommend particular wines with particular dishes.

Bring your own Some restaurants allow diners to bring their own wine. The restaurant may charge corkage to cover the cost of glasses and serving, but you will make a significant saving in the long run and you can be sure that you will enjoy your meal with the wine of your choice.

WINE LISTS When a sommelier offers you a wine list, take time to read it thoroughly, and wait until you have chosen your food before making a final decision. Ask the sommelier for guidance if you are spoilt for choice.

Pronunciation

If you would like to try a wine that you cannot pronounce with confidence, point to it, or refer to it by the number on the menu. Otherwise, here is our guide on how to pronounce some well-known wines and wine terms.

Alsace	al-zass	**Clos**	kloh	**Pinot grigio**	pee-no-gree-jee-oh
Amontillado	ah-mon-tee-yah-doh	**Cuvée**	koo-vay	**Pouilly Fuissé**	poo-yee-fwee-say
Beaujolais	boh-zhuh-lay	**Chenin**	shur-nan	**Rhône**	rone
Beaune	bone	**Claret**	klar-rett	**Riesling**	reece-ling
Brouilly	broo-yee	**Côte**	koht	**Rioja**	ree-yok-ah
Brut	brute	**Côteaux**	kot-toh	**Rosé**	ro-say
Cabernet	kab-er-nay	**Domaine**	doh-mayn	**Quincy**	can-see
Chablis	shab-lee	**Frascati**	fras-kart-tee	**Saumur**	soh-muhr
Chardonnay	shar-don-nay	**Graves**	grahv	**Sauvignon**	saw-vee-nyon
Châteauneuf du Pape	sha-toh-nurf-doo-pap	**Hermitage**	er-mee-tahj	**Semillon**	seh-mee-yon
		Macon	ma-kon	**Soave**	swah-vay
		Madeira	ma-dee-rah	**Valpolicella**	val-pol-li-chel-lah
		Médoc	may-dok	**Verdelho**	ver-dell-loh
		Merlot	mehr-loh	**Vin de pays**	vin duh pay-ee
		Navarra	na-vah-rah	**Vinho Verde**	veen-yo-vaird
		Penedes	peh-neh-dez	**Viognier**	vee-oh-nyay

CHOOSING WINE FOR A GROUP *It can be difficult to choose wine for a group if everyone is eating different meals. Ask the group for ideas (you could ask for more wine lists if appropriate) and order at least one red, one white and plenty of mineral water.*

SELECTING YOUR WINE

Unless you are selecting a particular wine to try, choose your meal before you choose the wine to go with it. You can then be sure that your wine will complement your food (see pages 46–7). If you would like some help, ask the sommelier specific questions to get the most useful advice, such as:

- Which red will go best with the lamb?
- What does the Zinfandel taste like?
- We are considering No. 17 and No. 23 – which would you recommend?

How much to pay

All restaurants put a high markup on wine – 200 per cent tends to be the minimum. Don't expect to pay what you would in a shop, although most restaurants buy wine at wholesale prices. Some restaurants follow a policy of adding a flat rate mark-up, which has the advantage (for the consumer) of making expensive wines better value than inexpensive wines.

Do consider choosing the cheapest wine if it is the one you want. All the wines should be of good quality, so don't feel compelled to pick an expensive one. The best value wines tend to be from the New World, where wines are the most likely to be reliable at lower prices.

THE WINE PRESENTATION RITUAL

This is your opportunity to check that this is the wine you ordered, and that the wine isn't faulty. It is not an opportunity to try the wine to see if you like it.

Whether you are a guest or host, it can be embarrassing to be seen making a fuss in a restaurant, but if there is something wrong with the bottle of wine you have ordered, it is far better to get things sorted out than to drink and pay for a bottle that you cannot enjoy. You can't send a bottle back after you've drunk a substantial quantity of the wine, so use the presentation ritual (see opposite) to make a thorough assessment of the wine.

The wrong vintage

This is where mistakes often occur – simply because restaurants run out of one vintage and move onto another without updating the wine list. If the wine that you ordered was a particularly good year, and the next vintage was much less good in that region, you should certainly query it.

If the restaurant doesn't have the vintage you ordered, you may want to see the wine list again and choose something else. If, on the other hand, you have chosen something like a young white wine where the vintage makes little difference, you may choose to accept the new year.

Faulty wine

If you think there is something wrong with the wine, you could ask one of your party for a second opinion, or ask the sommelier to try it. If you agree that the wine is faulty, the sommelier should replace the bottle immediately, and you'll go through the same assessment process with another bottle of the same wine. You should not feel embarrassed – wine can be spoiled during bottling or transportation – the fault is unlikely to be attributable to the restaurant. They might even be able to claim back the value of the wine from their wholesaler.

■ If the sommelier thinks that the wine is not faulty, and it is the style of the wine, you have a choice. Do you back down and accept his or her judgement, or do you argue? This entirely depends on how sure you are of your judgement. It's an awkward moment, and there are no sure guidelines. Good sommeliers will avoid such potentially difficult situations by accepting the customer's judgement without question.

■ If the second bottle is also faulty, then don't be embarrassed to say so. You could make a joke of it, if you like – after all, it's unlikely to be the restaurant or sommelier's fault. At this point, you may want to choose another wine from the list.

■ It is extremely unlikely that the sommelier will bring the same bottle back, but do check the bottle to see if the capsule is in place. If it's not, point it out, and ask politely for another bottle.

■ If you've asked for a wine to be decanted and it has been done badly, so that you are getting deposit in the glasses, ask the sommelier to filter the wine. Don't worry if there are white crystals or pieces of cork in the wine – they are not a fault (see pages 80–81), but you could ask the sommelier to decant the wine.

The wrong temperature

A wine should be on a list only if it is ready to drink. In the same way, it should only be served at the right temperature. This can be a problem, particularly when drinking abroad, where tastes may be different. If a fine red wine is served at cellar temperature, the sommelier should have warned you that it will be colder than commonly accepted. If he or she can't warm it, then the sommelier should tell you what is available to drink at an appropriate temperature.

If a wine is too warm, ask for an ice bucket – this includes red wine as well as white. Give it a few minutes in the bucket to cool down before you pour. If your wine is in an ice bucket, help yourself, although a good sommelier should also anticipate when your glass needs refilling.

CHECKING WINE IN A RESTAURANT

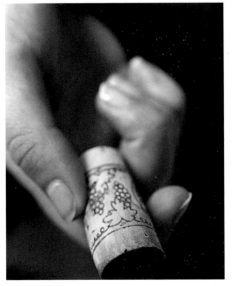

1 The sommelier will show you the unopened bottle. This is your opportunity to ensure that this is the exact bottle you ordered. Check that the vintage is the one you asked for.

2 Once you have accepted the bottle, the sommelier will uncork it and might show you the cork. Look to see if the cork is in good condition, and if it looks suspicious, smell the cork for mustiness. You can usually tell more by smelling the wine when poured.

3 The sommelier will pour a small amount of wine into the glass of the person who ordered it, or he or she may ask who would like to taste. If the table has ordered more than one wine, the sommelier may ask who would like to taste each bottle.

*Wine with*

DESSERTS

Whether serving a fresh fruit salad or a rich chocolate cake, you need to choose a wine that will round off your meal as beautifully as your dessert. Choose a wine that highlights the flavours of the dessert, and that is not overwhelmed by its consistency.

Chocolate

A chocolate-based dessert is difficult to pair with wine because of the extreme sweetness and its lavish texture, which can coat the palate. You need a wine to cut through both. (Port is also a good choice.)

Muscats Those from Australia are too powerful for most desserts, but work beautifully with rich chocolate.
Maury This French wine is a fabulous choice for almost all chocolate desserts.

Fruit

How you serve the fruit – fresh in a salad, baked in a tart or stewed – determines the type of wine you need. The texture, temperature and acidity level of the wine are what you need to consider.

Muscat-de-Beaumes-de-Venise Serve with plums or blackberries for a sensational combination.
Riesling A fruit tart works well with most of the sweet Rieslings.
Sauternes This complements the sharp flavour of rhubarb and apple.

Cream

Rich, creamy desserts can be difficult to match unless served with acidic fruit to cut through the mouth-coating texture. You need a wine that can cope with cloying consistency.

Semillon-Sauvignon Sweet blends from the New World have the flavour and concentration required for heavy, creamy desserts like cheesecake.
Sherry Choose a sweet sherry for drinking with custard-based desserts such as crème brûlée.

Cold

Ice creams and sorbets are the classic palate refresher at the end of a meal. Serve your chosen wine ice cold, too, to leave the palate tingling. Madeira makes a nice contrast.

Moscato d'Asti For ice-cold fruit sorbets, go for a wine with sweetness and sparkle.
Muscat To accompany vanilla ice cream, Muscat-de-Beaumes-de-Venise has the best consistency.

Hot

Freshly baked desserts are perfect for winter days. Serve with custard or ice cream, and a rich dessert wine or fortified wine.

Malmsey Madeira Good to pick up the richness of a hot treacle tart.
Chenin Blanc For a hot apple pie, choose a sweet style.
Sauternes Complements the fruitiness of rhubarb and apples, so serve with baked fruit desserts.

Cakes and gâteaux

Whether you are serving a light sponge cake or a dark, rich fruit cake, look for a wine that will lift the flavours and add moisture.

Champagne If you are serving cake as part of a special celebration, choose a special sparkling wine.
Coteaux du Layon For almond or marzipan cakes, this will enhance the nutty flavour and rich texture.
Muscat A rich fruit cake needs a wine with a generous amount of sweetness and strength.

SUMMER FRUITS WITH PASTRY LAYERS Serve with a chilled Muscat.

The vast array of corkscrews, glassware and wine gadgets available to the
wine enthusiast is an indication of how complicated serving wine can be.
In this chapter we look at the essentials of serving wine, and how you can
do justice to your wine without unnecessary fuss. We also explore the
etiquette of serving wine, whether you are the host or a guest.

The chapter includes: serving wine at the right temperature; how to
open wine bottles; pouring wine; and decanting and breathing. We move
on to choosing glassware to enhance your wine; laying the table; and how
to clean and care for glassware. The chapter ends with planning for a
special occasion, and looks at delicious wine-based drinks, including
several classic cocktails.

Serving

wine

GETTING THE *Temperature* RIGHT

Serving wines at the correct temperature allows them to show off their charms. Without being too dogmatic, white wine needs to be cool enough to be refreshing, while red wine should be slightly warmer. On a hot summer's day you may well prefer all wines to be slightly cooler than you would on a cold winter's evening.

RED WINE

If you have brought up a red wine from a cool cellar, it is best to let it warm up gradually rather than rapidly. This can take a few hours, however, so when possible, plan ahead. Over-heating a wine can kill its flavour, so if in doubt, serve it too cool: its temperature will soon rise in your hand or with the warmth of the dining room. To get red wine to the ideal temperature, choose one of the following options:

■ Stand the bottle in the kitchen for a couple of hours – it is invariably the warmest room in the house.

■ Put the bottle into a sink or bucket of warm water – a temperature of about 20°C (70°F) will warm the wine to 15–18°C (59–65°F) in about 8 minutes. Bear in mind that the label will probably come off.

■ You could use a wine warmer or *Therm au Rouge*. It is a similar shape to a rapid-chill sleeve. Place it into a saucepan of boiling water to heat, then slide over a bottle to warm the wine. Do not warm a bottle of red wine and then return it to the cellar. Fluctuating temperatures adversely affect wine (see pages 44–5).

Do not over-warm the wine or the wine will taste cloying.

what's in a name?

Chambré A French word for room temperature, often used to describe the correct temperature for serving red wine. The term is misleading, however – room temperature fluctuates and the word was coined at a time when the temperature in houses was cooler.

Wineometer

One type of wineometer resembles a regular thermometer which you place in the open bottle, and one type clips around the outside of the bottle. With the latter, the bottle need not be open, so you can check in advance.

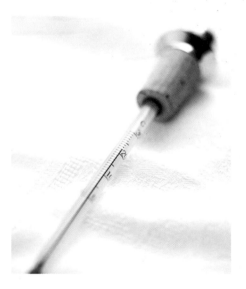

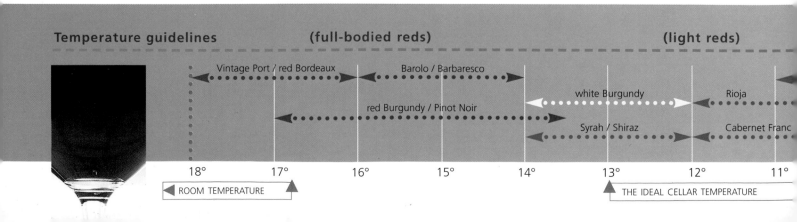

Temperature guidelines   (full-bodied reds)   (light reds)

Vintage Port / red Bordeaux   Barolo / Barbaresco

white Burgundy   Rioja

red Burgundy / Pinot Noir

Syrah / Shiraz   Cabernet Franc

18°   17°   16°   15°   14°   13°   12°   11°

◄ ROOM TEMPERATURE ►   ▲ THE IDEAL CELLAR TEMPERATURE

WHITE WINE

It is much easier to serve white wine at the right temperature than it is red – in some cases a wine straight from the cellar will be cool enough. Bear in mind that the higher the quality of a white wine, the less cold it should be served, so that you can properly appreciate its flavour. To get white wine to the right temperature, choose one of the following options:

▪ Store the bottle in the refrigerator for an hour before serving. Don't keep in the refrigerator for too long, however, as over-chilling could impair the flavour of the wine.

▪ Immerse the entire bottle in ice-cold water (see right) for 10 minutes. This is a more efficient method than the refrigerator, as water is a better cooling medium than air.

▪ In an emergency, you can place the bottle in the freezer for up to 15 minutes, although this is not recommended for fine wines. Keep checking on the wine so that it doesn't freeze.

▪ Many wine shops now have cooling machines that can chill a bottle in a few minutes, which is ideal for taking wine to a party.

Avoid over-chilling the wine, as this kills its flavour and aroma; over-warming on the other hand will leave the wine bland to taste.

Table-top coolers

Keep your bottle of white wine chilled between pourings using a cooling vessel. There are several types available:

Terracotta wine cooler Half an hour prior to use, fill with ice and water, then tip out just before you insert the bottle. The terracotta will remain cool for up to 2 hours and will look very attractive on your dinner table.

Plastic vacuum cylinder This works like a Thermos flask, keeping a chilled bottle cool by surrounding it with a vacuum.

Ice bucket Use to speed-chill a bottle or to keep a bottle cool once open (see below).

Rapid-chill sleeve Keep it in the freezer, then slide it over the bottle.

USING AN ICE BUCKET

1 Fill the bucket with a mixture of ice and cold water. (Always use water – ice cubes or crushed ice are not enough on their own.) Place the unopened bottle upside down in the water for 2–3 minutes. Turn and chill for a further 2–3 minutes to ensure that the whole bottle is cooled.

2 Return the bottle to an upright position and chill for a further 5 minutes. Turn the bottle in the bucket occasionally to ensure the entire bottle is kept chilled. To serve, wrap a napkin around the bottle to prevent drips, pour, and return the bottle to the bucket to stay cool.

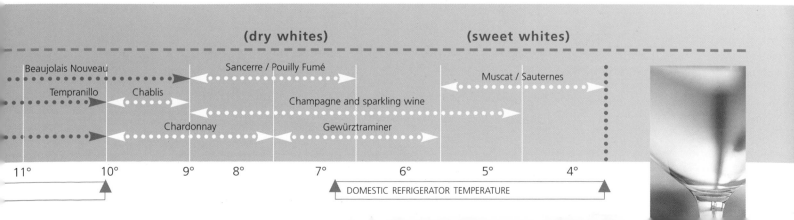

(dry whites)　　　(sweet whites)

Beaujolais Nouveau

Sancerre / Pouilly Fumé

Muscat / Sauternes

Tempranillo　　Chablis

Champagne and sparkling wine

Chardonnay　　Gewürztraminer

| 11° | 10° | 9° | 8° | 7° | 6° | 5° | 4° |

DOMESTIC REFRIGERATOR TEMPERATURE

CHEESE

Wine and cheese events are very popular, but the two are actually very hard to match successfully – the strong flavour and texture of cheese can overpower most wines. If serving cheese at the end of a meal, choose just one good cheese, and one delicious wine to go with it.

Cream and soft cheese

Brie, Camembert and cream cheese are difficult to marry with wine · because of their mouth-coating textures. Sparkling wines have a palate-cleansing effect that works well with these cheeses.

Champagne The tangy taste of soft cheese works well with a yeasty Champagne. The bubbles cut through the creamy mouthfeel.
Chardonnay A mature bottle tempers the lactic acid in cheese, enhancing the creamy textures.

Goat's cheese

It can be difficult to find wine to complement the notable, attractive acidity of goat's cheese. Serve with salad leaves, apple and fennel to temper the cheese, and offer a fruity wine that has low acidity.

Grenache This spicy, fruity red is an ideal companion.
Sancerre A classic match with goat's cheese – the crisp wine complements the creamy, rich cheese.

Blue cheese

Strong-flavoured blue cheeses have a very distinctive flavour. Choose a rich dessert or fortified wine for an incredible, rich, mouthfeel.

Sauternes A glass of chilled dessert wine is a taste sensation with creamy blue cheese. Serve with slices of ripe pear at the end of a meal.
Port Serve vintage or tawny port to contrast with a firm, flavoursome blue cheese, to temper its pungency.
Hermitage This robust, rich red will stand up to strong-flavoured cheese.

Semi-hard cheese

Cheddar and other semi-hard cheeses require a mature wine to bring out the flavours of both. An aged Semillon suits most semi-hard cheeses. Dry oloroso sherry is also a good choice.

Semillon The aromas of butter and toast in this wine enhance the creamy texture of semi-hard cheeses.
Port This is the classic accompaniment to most cheese, and goes particularly well with strongly flavoured ones.

Hard cheese

Parmesan, Pecorino and Sapsago are all strong-flavoured, hard cheeses, used mostly for shaving and grating. They are best matched with robust red wines. If this type of cheese is being used as a garnish, it might be more appropriate to match the wine to the main ingredient of the dish.

Italian red wine Take your lead from the makers of the finest hard cheeses in the world, and serve with robust Barolos and Chiantis.

Smoked cheese

The salty, bacon taste of smoked cheese is so distinctive that it is very difficult to find a wine that can live up to it, without altering the flavour of the wine for the worse.

Sauternes You need a sweet dessert wine to withstand the smoky flavour.
Gewürztraminer Choose one that is full-bodied enough to cope.
Shiraz Try an Australian Shiraz, which is sweeter and richer than the Syrah of the Rhône.

GOAT'S CHEESE, ROCKET AND WALNUT SALAD Choose a fruity red wine such as Grenache to accompany rich goat's cheese.

Opening A WINE BOTTLE

There are few sounds more evocative than the soft pop of a cork coming out of a bottle – followed, of course, by the glug–glug of wine being poured. If you're the one doing the bottle opening, you'll want to make sure that the experience is as relaxing for you as it is for everyone else. Here is how to ensure smooth access to your wine.

GETTING STARTED

There is a wide range of gadgets available to wine enthusiasts, but how many are actually necessary? This rather depends on how much wine you open, and how much you care about the appearance of the bottle after opening. In this section, we take you through each stage, suggesting ways to make opening a bottle as simple as possible.

CORKS AND CAPS

Wine bottles come with different types of stoppers, with corks the most widely used.

Cork This is the traditional closure and is made out of the stripped bark of the cork oak, *Quercus suber*. As with any natural product, the quality varies; they can be affected by TCA (see pages 80–81). It is the unpredictable nature of TCA, more than any other factor, that makes some people wary of corks: TCA-affected corks look the same as non-affected ones. You can only tell the difference by tasting the wine.

Plastic (or "synthetic") corks These are a recent innovation, and are becoming ever more popular with producers and consumers alike. You remove them in exactly the same way you would a traditional cork. They are more reliable and durable than traditional corks.

Stopper corks Used for some fortified wines that you can store standing up rather than lying down. They are made from cork with the addition of a plastic top that you can grip. Twist and lift to remove the cork.

Screw caps These are airtight, keep the wine very fresh and are easy to remove and replace. Research has shown that they are as effective as corks at storing wine, but commercial producers rarely use them, because they think consumers won't like them.

SCREW TYPES Corkscrew design has developed over the centuries – modern versions are designed to remove corks with great ease, and look good into the bargain. Experiment with different designs to find one to suit you.

OPENING A BOTTLE OF STILL WINE

1 Place the bottle on a table. Remove the top of the capsule to reveal the top of the cork. Some capsules have a tear tag. If not, use the point of a corkscrew or use a foil cutter (see below, right).

2 Place the point of the corkscrew in the centre of the exposed cork and push. Hold the corkscrew and bottle firmly, and rotate the corkscrew until the helix is submerged in the cork.

3 If using a Screwpull (as pictured), continue to rotate the corkscrew to lift the cork out of the bottle neck. For other types of screw, follow the instructions below and overleaf.

BOTTLE STOPPERS Natural cork (left) is the traditional material used for bottle closures, but plastic corks (right) are gaining in popularity.

Foil cutters

The top of the bottle is covered with foil or plastic wrapping (a "capsule") that needs to removed before pulling the cork. A foil cutter is very useful if you are opening a large quantity of bottles or want to remove the top of the capsule neatly. Place the cutter over the top of the bottle and turn.

CORKSCREWS

There are various gadgets on the market – some of which are more effective than others – and everyone has their own preference. Here are some of the most common corkscrews and tips on how to use them:

Basic corkscrew This is just a screw and a handle. Twist the helix (or spiral) into the cork, and hold the bottle steady. Grasp the handle and pull out the cork. This is quite difficult to master, and requires strength.

Waiter's friend Screw the helix in and lever the cork out of the bottle by resting the spur on the arm on the lip of the bottle. The technique requires practice, but most sommeliers swear by them. Particularly good for bottles with a flange-top (see page 125).

Screwpull (see above) This is the simplest and most foolproof of all corkscrews. Slip over the neck of the bottle and screw the helix in. Simply keep on turning the handle in the same direction to lift the cork.

119

Lever screwpull A variation on the screwpull, this has two handles that you squeeze together to grasp the neck of the bottle and a lever that you lift to bring out the cork.

Double-screw corkscrew Screw the helix into the cork and then lift the cork out slowly with the counter-screw handle.

Twin-lever (or "wing") corkscrew As you screw the helix in, two levers gradually rise. Push down both levers firmly to lift the cork.

Two-pronged (or "thief") corkscrew This is known as a "thief" because, in theory, you can remove the cork without making a hole, replace the wine with water, and put the cork back. In practice, this is unlikely, as corks expand after removal and seldom go back into a bottle completely. You use this corkscrew by inserting the thin prongs down the side of the cork, between the cork and the bottle neck. You'll need to use a see-saw motion to ease the prongs in. Once in, pull firmly to remove the cork.

THE LATEST CORKSCREW DESIGNS *Clockwise from top right: the Waiter's friend; a double-screw corkscrew; a basic corkscrew; and the twin-lever (or "wing") corkscrew. There are many fashionable variations of these basic designs, but they work in essentially the same way.*

OPENING A BOTTLE OF SPARKLING WINE

1 Hold the bottle at a 45 degree angle, pointing it away from your body. Put one hand over the cork and unscrew the wire cage with the other. Remove the cage carefully, keeping one thumb over it, so that if the cork starts to emerge, you can control it.

2 Ensure that your hand covers and holds the cork securely, so that it doesn't shoot out. Twist the bottle (not the cork) slowly while holding the cork steady. If you twist the cork rather than the bottle, you risk the head of the cork breaking off in your hand.

3 Ease the cork out slowly, covering it with the palm of your hand. Just as it starts to come out, push the cork to slow it down. It should come out with a sigh rather than a loud pop. If it is stubborn, use a bar towel for extra grip on the bottle.

Cork Troubleshooting

No matter how carefully you treat them, corks often get stuck or break. Because they are natural products, they may have flaws, have been badly made, or have deteriorated over time. Stuck corks are frustrating (see right) and often become broken ones, which in turn end up as pieces floating in your wine. Cork in the glass won't actually harm the wine or affect the flavour, but it is best avoided when possible.

BROKEN CORKS

Sometimes a cork breaks off as you're pulling it out, leaving you with half a cork still in the bottle. If the piece is large enough, you could try to remove it with the corkscrew. Position the corkscrew (ideally, the Waiter's friend) at a 45 degree angle and lever out as normal. This is effective in most cases and will bring out the remainder of the cork intact. For a smaller piece of cork, however, it may be difficult to insert the helix and you might find it easier simply to push the cork into the wine.

If you have pushed the cork right into the wine and it is still intact, hold it down with a long skewer and pour the wine into a decanter or jug. Alternatively, you

---

dislodging stuck corks

Often, you only discover the cork is stuck because the corkscrew goes straight through it. The cork is then too damaged for you to try again. In this situation you could:
- Try gently pushing the cork into the bottle. Since it has been stuck until now, it will probably offer some resistance, so be careful to avoid splashing.
- Run hot water over the neck of the bottle for 2–3 minutes to make the glass expand, and try to push the cork into the bottle.
- Ease a thin, sharp knife between the cork and the bottle neck. Loosen the cork or cut it into pieces.

---

could use a cork retriever (see below). If the cork has fragmented, you could decant the wine to ensure that you don't get pieces of cork in the glasses.

USING A CORK RETRIEVER

1 Slide the metal ring to the top of the retriever, about 3 cm (1 in) from the handle. Insert the legs into the bottle, and release the ring to open the legs. Grip the cork. The cork will probably be floating on its side, and you will need to grip it lengthways.

2 To hold the grip on the cork, move the ring down the legs as you lift the cork out of the bottle. Even if the cork is lying lengthways, you should be able to pull it out of the bottle neck.

Red Bordeaux and Tuscan wines

These, the richest of reds, from the great wine-producing areas of Bordeaux and Tuscany, need to be served with succulent foods that can pick up on their delicate flavours. Consider the age of the wine as well – this will influence your food choice.

WE RECOMMEND	
Red meat	● ● ● ● ●
Pasta	● ● ● ●
White meat	● ● ●
Fish	● ●
Vegetarian dishes	● ●

Red Bordeaux

With a young red Bordeaux wine, serve a dish with big flavours. The wine has berry overtones, which you can reflect in the sauces you serve with your meal – a redcurrant jus with roast squab and celeriac mash, for example.

An older red Bordeaux (eight to ten years in age) is mellower, but still exhibits some fruity characteristics. Serve with pan-fried red meat and aromatic vegetables or roast duckling with figs wrapped in Parma ham. The fruitiness of the figs and the nuttiness of the ham will complement both the rich meat and the wine.

Wines that are older than ten years have a very different range of characteristics – they can appear to be dull at first, but they come to life pleasantly on the palate. Choose food that has a compatible texture – gently roasted fillet of beef is very good with older red Bordeaux (see opposite). Use a younger (and less expensive) Bordeaux for the jus.

Tuscan wines

Perhaps the most famous of the Tuscan wines are Chianti and Chianti Classico. The former is larger than life; the latter more restrained and passive. Choose robust, classic Italian dishes or rich meat canapés to serve with Chianti.

With a young Chianti, Osso Bucco (veal knuckle braised with tomatoes, onions and garlic) picks up on the fruitiness of the wine. For a Classico, rich tomato stews and meat-based pasta dishes are excellent companions.

FILLET OF BEEF WITH MUSHROOM SAUCE

Rich, tannic red wines need strongly flavoured and textured red meat to complement them. Succulent tenderloin with earthy-tasting mushrooms brings out the richness of the wine.

SERVES 4

25 g (1 oz) butter
150 ml (5 fl oz) olive oil
500 g (1 lb 2 oz) beef fillet
500 ml (18 fl oz) robust red wine
500 ml (18 fl oz) veal stock
15 g (½ oz) cold butter, diced
salt and pepper, to taste
100 g (4 oz) enoki mushrooms
100 g (4 oz) shiitake mushrooms
100 g (4 oz) button mushrooms
300 g (10 oz) mixed wild mushrooms
  (such as oyster, chanterelle, girolle,
  moussonon, pied de mouton)

Preheat the oven to 180°C (350°F/gas 4).

Heat the butter and 100 ml of the oil in a large, shallow pan and fry the beef fillet for 1 minute on both sides to seal the edges. Transfer the beef to the oven and roast for 20–25 minutes. Remove from the oven and let rest for 5 minutes.

In a saucepan, bring the red wine to a gentle simmer and reduce by about 80 per cent. Add the veal stock and continue to simmer the mixture until the liquid has reduced by half. Remove from the heat and whisk in the cold butter. Season, and strain the sauce through a sieve.

Heat the remaining oil in a pan and lightly sauté all the mushrooms until they have just wilted.

To serve, slice the beef into four portions, place each slice in the centre of a plate, garnish with the mushrooms and then spoon the sauce around and over the beef.

Pouring Wine

Whether you are planning a formal sit-down dinner or just inviting a few friends around for a drink, it is good to know that you are doing justice to the wine – and to your guests – by serving your wine in the correct way. Pouring wine without spills is a knack worth learning.

POURING ETIQUETTE

When you have opened a bottle of wine, checked it for faults and decanted it, if necessary, you are ready to pour (see below). If it's an informal occasion, you can pour wine for your immediate neighbours and leave the bottle on the table for guests to serve themselves. For more formal dinners, you may want to take the bottle around the table yourself. Start by serving the most senior lady and then move around the table in a clockwise direction. Stand behind each person to his or her right-hand side as you pour – don't reach across your guests. Serve yourself last.

Being a good host

At any occasion, the most important thing is to look after your guests and make sure they have enough to drink, without pressing wine on them. People like to

pouring sparkling wine

- Your success pouring Champagne or sparkling wine will depend on how you have opened the bottle (see page 120). If the wine is over-agitated, leave it to rest for a few moments until any frothing stops.
- Hold the glass at a 45 degree angle to keep the froth under control and straighten it gradually as you pour.

drink at different rates – even if you drink slowly, you should not forget to refill your guests' glasses. However, it can be difficult for people to keep tabs on how many glasses they've consumed if their host is constantly topping up their glasses. It's much better to allow somebody to empty his or her glass, or nearly empty it, before offering them some more. Don't pour into somebody's glass without asking the person first. For informal occasions, it is best to place the wine within easy reach and to let your guests help themselves as and when they feel like it.

POURING STILL WINE

1 Hold the glass upright, or stand the glass on the table – there is no need to tilt a glass for still wine. Hold the bottle in the middle and lower the bottle to near the glass.

2 Position the lip of the bottle about 1 cm (½ in) above the glass, just off-centre of the glass. Tilt the bottle gently to pour in a steady stream.

3 When you finish pouring, twist the bottle towards you slowly above the glass before you take it away, to minimize dripping.

DEALING WITH SPILLS AND STAINS

However carefully you pour your wine, the occasional spillage is inevitable at dinners and parties. Sometimes spilled wine can cause long-lasting damage to soft furnishings, carpets, clothes and furniture if not dealt with promptly, so act quickly.

Dry white wine will not stain most fabrics. For white wine spills on carpets or upholstery, mop up quickly using absorbent kitchen paper and the stain should disappear. You may, however, need to use a cloth and some soap to remove the smell. For spills on clothing, dab with kitchen paper and wash as normal.

Spilled red wine, however, can be a real problem. There are several theories about what will remove red wine stains, but their success varies according to the type of fabric and the darkness of the red wine – the darker and more tannic the red wine, the more likely it is to leave a stain.

Cleaning up red wine

Dry white wine This can be a remarkably effective remedy for red wine stains. Dab white wine onto a carpet or upholstery liberally with a cloth or immerse an item of clothing in a bowl of white wine. Rinse thoroughly in cool water and then wash as normal.

Salt Some people swear by sprinkling salt onto red wine spills on carpets. This may be effective for soaking up some of the liquid, but it does little to counteract staining.

Washing If you get red wine on your clothes, rinse the affected area in cold water to remove as much of the wine as possible. Stubborn stains may come out during a machine wash, especially using a good-quality washing powder. Some dark red wines, however, may leave behind a pale blue stain.

Stain removers If the affected material is colourfast and washable, you could use one of the branded products specially made to deal with red wine; they are generally remarkably effective. Keep a bottle of stain remover at home in case of accidents, as immediate treatment is most effective.

Dry cleaning For unwashable material, you could try taking it to the dry cleaners and telling them that the stain is red wine. If the fabric is not colourfast, however, you may find that it's beyond rescue.

FLANGE-TOPS *The Robert Mondavi winery, California, pioneered the flange-top bottle neck. Many wine producers have adopted the design for their own bottles. The lip reduces drips and replaces the need for a drip-stopper or foil disc (see below).*

Pouring gadgets

Drip-stopper A metal pourer that fits over the top of the bottle and catches drips inside.
Wine collar A ring lined with absorbent material. It slips over the bottle neck and catches drips inside.
Foil disc These discs of plastic-coated foil are often used at trade wine tastings, and pour wine cleanly.

Red Burgundy and Pinot Noir

The pinot noir grape is the base for Burgundy wines, but the grape is also cultivated elsewhere, producing wines with different features. Elusive, rich, and intriguing, all of the pinot noir wines require fine foods that will do them justice.

WE RECOMMEND	
Poultry	● ● ● ● ●
Game	● ● ● ● ●
Fish and seafood	● ● ●
Red meat	● ● ●
Summer fruits	● ● ●

Red Burgundy

The most opulent of wines are red Burgundies – scented on the nose, seductive in colour and leaving a hint of spice on the palate. As the pinot noir grape is one of the most difficult grapes to handle in winemaking, its Burgundies can be expensive. They are sometimes delicate, light in body and quite acidic, but they always deliver a surprising palate punch – do not be deceived by the fruity berry nose and the lightness of colour.
The ideal partners for a red Burgundy are game birds such as duck, particularly if they are served with stewed cherries, which pick up on this aspect of the wine's nose.

Other choices include roast guinea fowl with a mushroom sauce, or veal knuckle, roasted and finished with a truffle essence jus. Burgundy and truffle is a great combination.

For a wonderful taste sensation, try a young red Burgundy accompanied by fresh raspberries.

Pinot Noir

The Pinot Noir wines of the New World are riper than those from France and vary from medium- to full-bodied, with good palate length and big flavour. An aged New World Pinot Noir is great with fish, particularly salmon and tuna. For a special occasion, try a lobster dish with mushrooms in a creamy sauce.

Californian Pinot Noirs with their luscious fruity flavours can be matched successfully with most simple poultry dishes.

PAN-FRIED PIGEON WITH RED CABBAGE

Pigeon has a very distinctive flavour, which is brought out beautifully by the complex flavours of red Burgundy and Pinot Noir.

SERVES 4

50 g (1½ oz) sultanas
250 ml (9 fl oz) ruby port
3 tbsp redcurrant jelly
50 ml (2 fl oz) red wine vinegar
1 small red cabbage, finely shredded
500 ml (18 fl oz) game stock
salt and pepper, to taste
breasts and legs of 2 pigeons (about 280 g/10 oz each)
50 g (1½ oz) butter
50 ml (2 fl oz) olive oil
12 small Charlotte potatoes, peeled and boiled until tender
4 sprigs rosemary, deep-fried
2 cinnamon sticks, halved
20 redcurrants

Place the sultanas and a quarter of the port into a saucepan and simmer until reduced by half. Add the jelly and vinegar and stir until the jelly is melted. Add the cabbage and simmer for 30 minutes.

In another pan, heat the remaining port and simmer until reduced by half. Add the stock, reduce by half again, season and keep warm.

Pan fry the pigeon in the butter and oil for about 5 minutes, until golden brown all over. Remove from the pan and let rest for 5 minutes.

To serve, divide the cabbage into four, and pile in the centre of each plate. Slice the breast and arrange with the legs as pictured. Place the potatoes next to the pigeon and drizzle the port jus around the edge of the plate. Garnish with the redcurrants, cinnamon and rosemary.

Decanting and Breathing

Generally speaking, people worry about decanting more than is necessary. Few wines actually need to be decanted, and not all red wines need to breathe. But that doesn't mean you can't decant them if you want to. A beautiful decanter full of wine is a fine sight and will put your guests in a mood of eager anticipation.

There are two practical reasons for decanting wine. One is to separate the wine from any deposit it may have thrown during its long maturation in the bottle; the other is to allow the wine to aerate or "breathe". This encourages the development of the wine's bouquet and flavour. A common mistake is that people store wine in decanters – a wine will deteriorate if left in a decanter for more than a few hours.

Which wines need decanting?
It follows from the above that the only wines you need to decant are those which have spent a long time in the bottle. This includes top-class red Bordeaux and Cabernet Sauvignons, red Rhônes, Shiraz, red Burgundies, Barolos and other top Italian reds and vintage port.

If you want to check if the wine has thrown a deposit, hold the bottle up against a light source: if there's a dark stain on the inside of the glass where the bottle has been lying down, then it has thrown a deposit. Alternatively, you may see dark particles at the bottom of the wine.

■ *Red wine that is less than five years old does not need decanting. A fine young red wine may, however, benefit from having a short time to breathe.*

■ *There is no need to decant white wine. Prolonged exposure to air will spoil any fresh flavours.*

When is the time to decant?
Generally it is better to allow too little time than too much. Very old, frail wines will start to oxidize within an hour, and will spoil quickly. Err on the side of caution – if when you serve a wine you think it needs more time to breathe, pour it out and it will change quickly in the glass.

The most convenient time to decant is probably just before your guests arrive, which normally seems to be about an hour before you want the wine. That will be enough for most wines, and should not be too dangerous for old ones.

DECANTING FOR DISPLAY Wine looks wonderful in a well-designed decanter such as this crystal, stoppered decanter from Riedel.

How long will wine last in a decanter?

Do not store wine in a decanter. Even robust wines such as vintage port shouldn't be left in a decanter: port takes a while to show signs of oxidation, but it starts to lose its aroma within days.

Plan to finish a decanter in one go. Failing that, pour the remains into a clean, empty wine bottle and use one of the preserving methods on pages 140–1.

Breathing in the bottle

Opening a bottle of wine one to two hours before serving allows it to breathe. This is enough for most wines and easier for the sort of occasions when you don't want to bother with a decanter.

Decanting equipment

Funnels Place a funnel in the neck of your decanter to prevent wine being spilled. They are available in a range of materials including silver. Otherwise, a plastic kitchen funnel will do the job just as well. **Cradle** An expensive piece of equipment designed to tilt the bottle evenly and gently as you decant.

HOW TO DECANT

1 Stand the bottle upright 24–48 hours before decanting. Uncork the bottle carefully. Position a lamp nearby. Hold the decanter at the neck of the bottle, and pour gently and steadily.

2 As you get towards the last of the wine you'll see the sediment moving down the bottle towards the neck. Watch it closely: stop pouring just before the sediment leaves the bottle.

3 If you do not have a steady hand, or want to extract every last drop of wine, use a decanting funnel. Place the funnel in the neck of the decanter, and pour in the wine. The funnel will catch the sediment.

Decanter design

In the last 250 years, decanter design has changed very little. Decanters tend to be made of clear glass, without a handle and with a stopper.

Spirit decanters tend to be square. It's not usual to use these for wine, but it will certainly not harm the wine.

19th-century decanters often have a round bowl and a long straight neck. These are inexpensive and widely available.

18th-century decanters usually have sloping shoulders and straight or very gently convex sides.

Ship's decanters have wide, splayed bases to make them more stable.

Modern designs can take many different forms.

CHOOSING THE *Right Glass*

The right glass can make an enormous difference to your enjoyment of a wine. In particular, the shape can affect the way a wine tastes. Glasses that have been specially designed to enhance the flavour of wine aren't necessarily more expensive – sometimes wrongly shaped, over-ornate glasses can cost more, while doing absolutely nothing for your wine.

GLASS DESIGN

If you have taken the trouble to choose a wine with an interesting aroma and flavour, do it justice by serving it in a glass that will bring out its features. Choose a glass that tapers at the top (tulip-shaped), which allows the wine to release its aroma and will funnel the wine onto your tongue when you drink it. If you want to see the colour of the wine, choose a glass made of clear glass or crystal with no cutting, colour or other decoration, which will distort the colour of the wine. A tulip-shaped glass is sufficient for all wines – it will even do for Champagne and sparkling wine. Ideally, choose glasses that are quite thin – they are the most comfortable in the mouth.

If you want to branch out a little, invest in separate glasses for red, white and sparkling wine. Keep to the basic tapered shape, but try a larger glass for red wine, which has more room in the bowl for the aroma to develop. For Champagne or sparkling wine, use tall flutes that will emphasise the streams of bubbles. Choose a tapered design so that the bubbles do not dissipate too quickly.

tumblers and Paris goblets

Some bars and cafés in Europe serve wine in glasses that, strictly speaking, aren't the right shape. They won't particularly enhance the flavour of a wine, but they are perfectly adequate for everyday drinking. Tumblers are ideal for outdoor use – they are easy to pack and set down and are inexpensive to replace.

TULIP-SHAPED GLASSWARE A glass that tapers at the top is ideal for serving most wines. It enables you to swirl wine without spilling it, and has room in the bowl for the aroma of the wine to develop.

There are various glasses that you should avoid:
- Those that flare out at the rim, as the aroma will be dissipated away from the glass.
- Small glasses that do not allow room for the aroma of the wine to develop in the bowl.
- Those made of coloured, painted or cut glass because decoration distorts the colour of the wine in the glass.

SPECIALIST GLASSES

Some of the leading glass manufacturers, notably Riedel, whose glasses we describe here, make glasses for every type of wine – but are all these shapes necessary? Wine does taste different according to the glass in which it is served – if you taste the same Chardonnay in a narrow flute and in a large red wine glass, you will notice the difference. Manufacturers explain that this is because the different shapes funnel the wine onto different areas of your tongue, focusing the key flavours of the wine where you will taste them most. For example, the shape of a Riedel Riesling glass funnels the wine to the tip of the tongue to emphasise its crisp, fruity flavour, then passes the wine over the back of the tongue giving a long finish.

Most of us can manage without each type of glass – a basic tapered style is sufficient for most wines. If you particularly like one or two kinds of wine, however, it may be worth buying specialist glasses for those wines.

Choosing specialist glassware

Chardonnay glass A tapered shape that enhances freshness and allows mature white wines to express their full range of flavour.

Riesling glass Enhances the fruit and balance of this light, acidic wine. The lip allows the wine to pass straight to the tip of the tongue – emphasising sweetness and fruitiness.

Bordeaux glass The large bowl of this glass intensifies the flavour, aroma and texture of Cabernet Sauvignon and other Bordeaux wines. The shape also prolongs the finish of the wine.

Burgundy glass Enhances the fruit, acidity and balance of good Pinot Noir or Burgundy. The bouquet of the wine has room to develop in the bowl and the slight flare of the lip directs the fruity flavours onto the front of the palate.

Champagne glass Brings out the bouquet, creaminess and richness of good Champagne. Also emphasises a stream of bubbles, rising up the glass.

IDENTIFYING GLASSWARE You can buy glasses designed specifically for individual styles of wines. These are just a few examples from over thirty different glass designs for different wine styles. From left to right: Chardonnay, Riesling, Bordeaux, Burgundy, Champagne.

Laying the Table

Serving a formal dinner can be somewhat daunting, especially when you are planning to give your guests several courses, with a different wine for each. It helps to follow a few basic guidelines, to ensure that your settings are as clearly laid and easy to negotiate as possible. The same principles apply when you are faced with several glasses at a formal function or restaurant.

GLASS SETTING

When you are setting the table, place each person's glasses above and to the right of his or her knives. If you are serving only one wine, one wine glass and a glass for water are sufficient. If you do not have a wide range of glasses, choose the ones best suited to the wine you have (see pages 130–1).

If you are serving a number of courses with a different wine for every course, you will need a glass for each wine. You could change them with each course, but in a home environment it would be far simpler to set them on the table. You can place them as you choose, or use one of the following settings:

Arranging glassware

Triangle – three glasses The glass on the far right should be used first and the triangle should be followed around in an anti-clockwise direction.

Square – four glasses In this case, the first wine is normally served in the glass at the bottom right of the square, the next in the glass at the top right and so on anti-clockwise.

Straight line – five glasses The glasses should be placed in order of use, from the outside in – just like cutlery. For example, the glass you will use first will be the one furthest to the right. A water glass should be the last glass – the one furthest to the left. The row of glasses is usually placed diagonally to the place setting, although some people prefer to have them horizontal to the place setting.

Order of serving

Wine should be served to correspond to the courses being served. If you are serving different wines for each course, you could remove the bottle, or suggest that everyone helps to finish it off. Don't remove a glass that has wine in it without checking with the guest.

Positioning bottles and decanters

Use common sense when deciding where to place bottles or decanters on a table. If you need to keep wine cool, think about whether you will need wine coolers, which may take up too much room, and may be better placed next to a table. You can buy wine cooler sleeves and jackets (see page 115), which fit the bottle snugly and do not take up too much room.

Clearing glassware

As a guest finishes each course, and his or her plate is cleared, you could remove the corresponding wine glass (provided it is empty). At the end of the meal, he or she should be left with just a dessert wine or Champagne glass and a water glass.

If you are serving sparkling wine or Champagne for a toast at the end of a meal, and if you have set glasses, check that they are still clean and available before you start to serve the wine – it is not unusual for guests to use the wrong glass. You may want to set out the Champagne flutes after the meal, to ensure that everyone has a clean, full glass for the toast.

If serving port, place port glasses to the right of the table setting, above where the knives were, for each guest. Coffee can be served directly in front of a guest.

ORDERING DRINKS *To make it easy for your guests to navigate a collection of wine glasses, place them in order of use, from right to left. You could arrange in a triangle; a square; or a straight line (clockwise, from top left).*

Hermitage, Côte Rôtie and Shiraz

The wines from the syrah grape, especially as grown in the Rhône Valley and in Australia (where it is known as shiraz) are very big in terms of colour, nose and flavour. They therefore call for foods with similar strength and texture.

Côte Rôtie

Another rich red with plenty of flavour and character. Sometimes white Viognier is added to the syrah, to create a slight muskiness.

As with Hermitage, try beef casseroles or roast game – particularly if you are serving an older wine. Wines of ten years or more develop a complexity that needs to be matched with rich, highly textured food.

The young Côte Rôtie wines lend themselves to veal and pork terrine-style dishes.

Hermitage

This famous wine made from the Northern Rhône syrah grape, has delicious spiciness, pepperiness and generous tannin. It is full-bodied and packed with flavour and needs a meaty, juicy accompanying dish.

Beef dishes that feature grilling or barbecuing are ideal – the crispiness and juiciness of the meat are texturally perfect. Serve with garlic butter or mustard sauce.

Hermitage also works well with some hard cheeses, particularly English ones.

Shiraz

The Australian version of Syrah, Shiraz, is a softer, more delicate wine than the French Syrah, and has greater fruitiness. Choose meats such as beef and venison or try a roast lamb dish with lots of extra flavour (see right).

Older Shiraz (10–15 years old) is ideal with the Christmas turkey. It is particularly delicious with the dark meat of the turkey and ideal with seasoned bread stuffing. There is just enough fruit in the aged wine to take on the cranberry sauce.

RACK OF LAMB WITH A HERB CRUST

Lamb has a tender consistency and rich flavour that enhance the texture of these delicious red wines.

SERVES 4

50 ml (2 fl oz) vegetable oil
2 racks of lamb, French trimmed
150 g (5½ oz) fresh white breadcrumbs
40 g (2 oz) parsley
1 egg
salt and pepper, to taste
30 g (1 oz) whole-grain mustard
12 small shallots
12 small cloves garlic, peeled
30 g (1 oz) brown sugar
50 g (1½ oz) cold butter, diced
100 ml (4 fl oz) ruby port
500 ml (18 fl oz) lamb stock
4 small sprigs thyme
4 small sprigs rosemary

Preheat the oven to 200°C (400°F/gas 6).

Heat the oil in a pan and sear the lamb until golden brown. Roast in the oven for 15–20 minutes, then remove.

In a food processor, blend the breadcrumbs, parsley and egg until fine, then season. Brush mustard onto the lamb and coat with the mixture.

Place the shallots and garlic onto a sheet of foil and sprinkle with the brown sugar and butter. Roast in the foil parcel for 15 minutes or until golden brown.

In a pan, bring the port and the lamb stock to the boil, simmer until it has reduced by half, and season.

Preheat the grill. Grill the lamb crust-side-up for 5 minutes. Let rest for 5 minutes and slice into cutlets.

To serve, place a quarter of the cutlets on each plate and arrange the shallots and garlic around. Drizzle the sauce around the plate and serve with a sprig each of rosemary and thyme.

Cleaning
GLASSES AND DECANTERS

Clean, sparkling glasses are essential for the full enjoyment of wine. It can take some time to clean glassware properly, but it is well worth the effort to keep glasses looking their best. Dishwashers have made the chore of glass cleaning easier, but if you own fine crystal glasses, it may be more prudent to wash them by hand.

CARING FOR GLASS AND CRYSTAL

As wine evaporates, it leaves a ring of residue. This is not usually a problem, but if crystal or glass is not cleaned fairly quickly, the wine will stain your glasses or decanter.

Most glasses can be put in a dishwasher (see opposite), and some glass manufacturers recommend it. Some wine glasses, however, are too tall to fit in the racks, and if you are worried about fragile crystal, you may prefer to wash them by hand (see below).

Decanters can be difficult to clean – you can't fit them into a dishwasher and their narrow necks make access difficult. They are, however, made from stronger, thicker glass than wine glasses, so they are easier to handle as you wash them.

Cleaning decanters

Always rinse out a decanter with warm water as soon as possible after use. Do not use detergent – it will be extremely difficult to get rid of any residue because of

WASHING GLASSES BY HAND

1 Fill the sink with warm water – there is no need to add detergent. Make sure the tap is out of the way. Wash one glass at a time using a lint-free linen cloth.

2 Rinse the glasses thoroughly under tepid running water to remove any traces of wine. Check the glass is clean by smelling the bowl of the glass.

3 To give the glasses a professional sparkle, hold them individually by the stem over a bowl of boiling water before drying, to steam the outside of the glasses.

4 Dry the glasses using a clean lint-free linen cloth. Hold the bowl of the glass with one hand while you dry it with the other. Don't hold the glass by the stem when drying the bowl, as you may break it.

5 Wrap a cloth around the handle of a wooden spoon to reach the bottom of the bowl, if necessary – pushing a cloth into the glass by hand may break the bowl.

the narrow neck of the decanter. To get into difficult areas, twist a damp linen cloth into a narrow rope, feed it in through the neck of the decanter and twist it around – use the handle of a wooden spoon to direct it into corners. Use a bottle brush to remove stubborn stains – choose nylon rather than wire, which can scratch.

If stains do build up, the traditional way to remove them is to put some lead shot into a decanter and shake it around. Alternatively, buy non-lead substitutes (see below), or you could use a solution of denture cleaning powder.

To dry a decanter, use a dry linen cloth twisted into a rope to reach difficult areas, or use a decanter drier. These are small muslin sacks of humidity-absorbing crystals. Place in a washed decanter and leave overnight or until all the excess water has been absorbed. These driers are very effective and can be re-used.

Cleaning balls

A modern-day substitute for lead shot, copper balls are used for removing wine stains from decanters.

WASHING GLASSES IN A DISHWASHER

1 Wash glasses in a separate cycle from other tableware to prevent particles of food from sticking to the glasses.

2 Stack the glasses with the bowl down. This prevents pools of water collecting in the bowls and minimizes any movement during the cycle.

3 Set the dishwasher on the shortest cycle. There is no need to use detergent or a rinse aid – most will leave a residue or a slight odour that will affect the appearance of the glass and the taste of wine over time.

4 Once the cycle is finished, open the door of the dishwasher. Leaving glasses in a humid atmosphere will tarnish them over time.

5 Dry the glasses with a lint-free linen cloth. Hold the bowl of the glass with one hand while you dry it with the other. Do not leave glasses to drip-dry, as water will smear them.

bartender tips

■ Glass absorbs smells, which can spoil the taste of a wine. The ideal way to store glasses is upright on an open shelf. This allows air to circulate around the glasses. Don't store glasses in a cardboard box or in an enclosed cupboard; they may pick up the smell of cardboard or other things stored in the cupboard.

■ To disperse any smells that may have accumulated, pass the glass quickly through the air a few times, to get fresh air into the bowl. If that doesn't work, try rinsing the glass with cold water or, if necessary, with a little of the wine you are planning to serve.

■ When drying glasses, make sure that the cloth you use is clean – stale or dirty cloth smells will transfer themselves to glassware. Cloths should be washed in normal detergent, but without fabric conditioner, which can leave a film.

■ Use lint-free linen cloths; cotton can shed loose fibres on your glassware.

Barolo and Barbaresco

These top-quality Italian reds made from the nebbiolo grape are high in alcohol and rich in flavour. They also are scented with beautiful flowery overtones and need to be accompanied by well-chosen dishes that can match their complexity.

WE RECOMMEND	
Red meat	● ● ● ● ●
Game	● ● ● ● ●
Pasta	● ● ● ●
Vegetarian dishes	● ● ● ●

Barolo

This is the nebbiolo wine with the most impact. It is heady and concentrated with high tannin and acidity levels, so it is well matched with luxurious food that can stand up to it. The perfect partner for a good bottle of Barolo is a rich beef dish, such as a succulent casserole or uncooked beef strips in a salad (see opposite). You also could serve the wine to accompany a flavoursome game stew. On the palate, the texture of well-hung game meat marries beautifully with the texture of a Barolo.

Barolo also responds well to a slightly lighter touch at the dinner table. A scented dish, such as fragrant couscous with a tagine of lamb is ideal. Other traditional Moroccan-style dishes often flavour lamb with rose water, which would be perfect to bring out the rose notes of the wine.

The sweetness of Barolo can sometimes be mistaken for fruit, but it is actually more of a chocolatey undertone. This kind of sweetness can work well with rich pasta dishes, provided they have enough sweetness of their own to complement the wine. Go for meaty pasta dishes such as a rich and chunky Spaghetti Bolognese.

Barbaresco

Lighter, drier and more aromatic than Barolo, Barbaresco is best served with rare roast beef or steak, or the distinctive flavours and textures of liver and kidneys.

Poultry also can work well when cooked appropriately – chicken in red wine with mushrooms and garlic, for example, or duck confit.

Barbaresco also suits pasta dishes. Choose hearty tomato sauces, rather than cream-based ones.

Vegetarian meals can be difficult to match with rich red wines, but Barbaresco is the exception – it is wonderful with roasted vegetables and couscous.

MELTED CARPACCIO OF BEEF

This classic Italian starter or light luncheon dish suits the robust flavours of these fine Italian reds.

SERVES 4

30 g (1 oz) wholegrain mustard
300 g (10 oz) beef fillet
75 g (3 oz) Parmesan cheese
175 g (6 oz) rocket, washed
24 black olives
24 sun-dried tomatoes
50 ml (2 fl oz) balsamic vinegar
100 ml (4 fl oz) olive oil
salt and black pepper, to taste
Parmesan cheese, shaved (optional)

Preheat the oven to 180˚C (350˚F/gas 4).

Brush the mustard onto the beef fillet and season with salt and pepper. Roll in cling film and place in the freezer until nearly frozen. (Partially freezing the meat makes it easier to slice.)

Remove from the freezer and, using a very sharp knife, slice the fillet wafer thin (you will need 6–8 slices per person). Arrange the meat onto a baking tray lined with baking parchment and return to the freezer.

Grate the parmesan finely. Sprinkle it into four circles, each about 10 cm (4 in) in diameter, on another baking tray lined with parchment. Bake for 5–7 minutes, until golden brown. Remove from the oven and leave to cool for about 1 minute. While still malleable, lift each circle with a palette knife, and shape into a cone.

Place a Parmesan cone in the centre of each plate and pile a portion of the rocket, olives and tomatoes around it. Whisk the vinegar and oil together to make a dressing and drizzle over the salad. Layer the beef slices around the plate on the salad. Season well. You could scatter some Parmesan shavings over the salad, to serve.

KEEPING WINE *Fresh*

Air and wine begin to react together the moment a bottle is opened. At first, air brings out the flavour and aroma of the wine, but if the wine is exposed to air for too long, it becomes oxidized (see pages 80–81). This is when the wine becomes flat, lacking in flavour and eventually completely spoiled. So how do you keep your wine at its best?

PRESERVING LEFTOVER WINE

The sooner you think about preserving wine you have just opened, the better. The less time oxygen has to get to work on the wine, the longer the wine will retain its flavour and aroma. Even using the best wine preserving gadgets on the market (see opposite), wine may not last for more than a week. A fine old wine may not last more than a few hours in any circumstance, and is best drunk as soon as possible.

If you leave the bottle open overnight, most wines will lose their aroma, and many will be spoiled. If you re-cork a bottle and leave it at room temperature, it should last 24 hours or more.

You have two options – preventing more air entering the wine, and removing air that has already entered the bottle.

Removing oxygen from a bottle

To do this effectively, use one of the many commercial gadgets that remove oxygen. These work on one of two principles – taking oxygen out of the bottle, or blanketing the wine with inert gas to prevent contact with oxygen. See above right for the two leading types.

CHAMPAGNE STOPPER *It is very hard to push a Champagne cork back into its bottle, as it expands on exit. To keep Champagne fresh and bubbly, use a stopper with a clamp attached to withstand the pressure caused by the carbonation.*

Preserving gadgets

Private Preserve A small canister of inert gas. You simply squirt it into the bottle and put the cork back in. This is a very effective preserving method.
Vacuum wine saver One of the simplest gadgets. It is a hand-operated pump that sucks the air out of the bottle. It comes with re-usable rubber stoppers (see right and below).
Wine bottle stopper Available in an assortment of designs, these work by preventing further air from entering the wine bottle (see far right). A cork will perform the same role.

Preventing further contact with air

■ *A re-corked bottle of wine (red or white) will keep for 2–3 days in a refrigerator. Place the bottle upright. You will need to warm up red wine before drinking it (see page 114).*
■ *If the cork is damaged, you could use a wine bottle stopper. Choose one with some "give" in the stopper part, so it can expand to make the bottle neck airtight.*

■ *If you have leftover wine in a decanter, rinse out the original bottle and pour the wine back in. Use one of the preserving methods listed above.*
■ *If you have less than half a bottle of leftover wine, pour it into a clean half-size bottle, and recork or stopper. It is a good idea to keep half-size bottles for this purpose, as the air to wine ratio is lower than if stored in a full-size bottle.*

Using a Vacuum Wine Saver

1 Wet the stopper with water first to make the seal secure. Push the rubber stopper into the top of the bottle – it should slip in easily.

2 Place the pump over the stopper and pump the handle up and down to remove the air. The pump will become difficult to move. Remove the pump, leaving the rubber stopper in the bottle.

staying bubbly

Sparkling wine lasts longer than any other wine because the carbon dioxide in the wine protects it from oxidation. Preserving the bubbles is the main concern. If you leave a bottle of sparkling wine open, it will take much longer to oxidize than still wine, but it will go flat quite quickly.

You do not want to create a vacuum, as this will make the wine go flat, but you can prevent more air from entering. It is very difficult to re-use the original cork, as it expands when removed. The best method is to use a stopper with a clamp attached. This prevents the pressure caused by the bubbles forcing the stopper out.

Alternatively, you can cut the original cork using a sharp knife until you can squeeze it into the bottle neck. Use the wire cage to hold the cork in place.

Many people claim that placing a teaspoon in the neck of a bottle of sparkling wine preserves the bubbles, but recent research has disproven this theory.

WINE *Etiquette*

Common sense prevails in all matters of etiquette, and this is certainly true when drinking wine. Customs, traditions and fashions change, and you might need to match your behaviour to suit your environment and the occasion. The following are guidelines (not rules) that may help to avoid embarrassment.

FORMAL OCCASIONS

If you are hosting a wedding, Christening, business dinner or other formal occasion, there is no need to provide a wide range of wines. If you do not provide a choice of menu, you do not need to provide a choice of wine – offer wine that best suits the food you are serving (see pages 46–7). If your menu would suit a choice of wine, then it is sufficient to offer one red and one white wine.

It is the host's responsibility to ensure that guests have enough wine, and that their glasses are filled. Unless wine is left on the table for you to help yourself, wait until offered.

A wine waiter will pour wine from your right-hand side. If you do not want wine, tell the wine waiter before he pours that you won't be having any wine. Do not turn your glass upside down, or pass an unused glass to the waiter. A wine waiter will remove glasses from your right-hand side. Food is served and removed from your left-hand side.

Table menus

If you are providing table menus, you could add details of the wine for interest. Include the year, grape or appellation and the name of the producer. List each wine under the course with which it will be served.

Drinking from the wrong glass

On pages 132–3 we explain the usual order of glassware on a table, which will help to avoid confusion, but if you use the wrong glass, it really doesn't matter. If another guest uses one of yours in error, do not draw attention to the mistake; simply ask the waiter for a new glass.

HOLDING A GLASS

When *tasting* wine at an organised tasting, hold the glass by the stem or the foot to look at the wine and swirl it (see page 71). This also prevents getting fingerprints on the bowl.

Most people hold the glass by the bowl when drinking *red* wine and brandy. The gradual warming by the hand will release the aroma of the wine, especially if the wine is slightly chilled.

Hold the glass by the stem when drinking *white* and sparkling wine, to avoid warming the wine. If your glass has been over-filled, however, you might find it easier to hold the glass by the bowl. Do whatever feels most comfortable.

GIVING WINE AS A GIFT *Wine is always a popular gift, especially Champagne. If you take wine to a dinner party, be aware that your host might have the wines worked out to match the food and may put your gift aside for a future occasion.*

passing the port

This is largely a British custom, and the reason behind it is lost in time. The host will produce the port, and usually serve the person on his right. The host will then serve himself, and pass it to the left. The port is then passed on to the left (clockwise) around the table.

When the port comes to you, help yourself and pass it on. If you don't want any, just pass it on – whatever you do, don't hold onto it. If you do, you might find cries of "Pass the port!" coming from the other side of the table. An alternative is "Do you know the Bishop of Norwich?" When you say that you don't know him, the retort comes back, "Well, he didn't pass the port, either".

toastmaster tips

- The host should be the first one to toast. For example, the father of the bride will usually make the first toast at a wedding, and a director at a corporate function.
- If you are the one making the toast, you will need to get everybody's attention first. You could tap your glass gently with a spoon, or ask the maître d' to call for silence; otherwise, stand up and ask everyone to be quiet, in a confident manner. There is no need to shout, but do repeat yourself if it is necessary.
- Follow the four *B*s for successful toasting: *be* upstanding, *be* sincere, *be* brief, and *be* seated.
- Stand when someone else calls a toast, unless otherwise specified.
- Clinking glasses was originally believed to drive away evil spirits, and it is still a popular custom today. Some people prefer to raise their glasses towards the person being toasted – either is acceptable, but you could see what others do first, if you choose.
- If you are the one being toasted, don't join in. It would, however, be polite to say a brief thank you.
- If you are unsure of a custom, do ask. Organisations such as universities may have unique customs.

Rioja and Tempranillo

The foods of the Rioja region are varied and range from sophisticated, highly flavoured dishes to more hearty, rustic fare. The indigenous wines of the region are equally adaptable, and can suit a range of dishes.

WE RECOMMEND	
Meat	● ● ● ● ●
Vegetables	● ● ● ●
Spicy foods	● ● ●
Fish	● ● ●

Rioja

Made predominantly from a blend of Spanish tempranillo and garnacha (also known as grenache) grapes, Rioja suits a variety of foods. A young Rioja tends to have good fruit, a lingering palate, and a flavour of oak, spice and strawberry, and would be ideal served with roasted lamb or pork – a traditional Riojan specialty. Another good match would be a *minestra* – a country-style vegetable stew topped with fried artichoke pieces. It has wonderful textures that sit beautifully with Rioja.

An older Rioja, say five or six years old, would suit a more robust roast lamb dish, baked with garlic and herbs. Spiciness and earthiness can be an enjoyable characteristic of this wine, so stewed dishes containing subtle spices would make a good accompaniment. Powdered caraway seeds mixed with cinnamon powder and sprinkled over a succulent breast of duck or over a chicken would result in a mouth-watering dish that, served with Rioja, would be a delight to the nose and palate.

Tempranillo

Wines made solely from the tempranillo grape are fruity, often with less use of oak than Rioja. They are suited to light red meat dishes, without a heavy sauce. Kidneys cooked with onions, garlic, a little mustard and splashed with red wine would be the perfect partner for a young tempranillo. A grilled lamb or pork steak served with a fruity sauce would highlight the fruit flavour of a Tempranillo. Baked mushrooms smothered in butter and chopped garlic would make an excellent accompaniment.

Seafood pies, made with a tomato sauce rather than a cream one, also go well. Game birds such as duck, served with a flavoursome fruit accompaniment (see opposite), and Tempranillo would be a wonderful combination. Pan-fried duck with roast onion marmalade would also work well.

CRISPY DUCK WITH GLAZED FRUIT

Serve a special Rioja with good fruit with this dish.

SERVES 2

1 duck
500 g (1 lb 2 oz) duck fat
1 Granny Smith apple, cut into wedges and fried (trimmings reserved)
30 g (1 oz) butter
400 ml (14 fl oz) duck stock
30 g (1 oz) caster sugar
200 ml (7 fl oz) orange juice
50 ml (2 fl oz) olive oil
2 bay leaves, deep-fried
8 glazed cherries, sautéed

Preheat the oven to 200˚C (400˚F/gas 6).

Remove the legs and breasts from the duck and trim and clean them. Cut the carcass into walnut-sized pieces and roast for 20–30 minutes.

In a large pan, heat the duck fat and deep fry the duck legs very slowly until crispy, approximately 50–60 minutes. Set aside.

Take the carcass from the oven, strain off the fat, and place the carcass in a large pan. Sauté the apple trimmings in butter and add to the pan. Add the stock, simmer for 30 minutes, strain and reserve the liquid.

Melt the sugar in a pan. Add the orange juice and reduce by half. Combine with the reserved stock.

Heat half the remaining butter and half of the oil and fry the duck breasts until golden. Transfer to the oven for 10 minutes, remove, and let rest for 5 minutes.

To serve, slice the duck breasts and arrange with the legs as shown. Garnish each plate with a bay leaf, fried apple and cherries, and drizzle with the stock jus.

145

PLANNING FOR A SPECIAL
Occasion

Whether you are organising a big formal occasion, or a simple family barbecue, a little pre-planning can help to make your event enjoyable for all – including the host. Here we look at how to choose the most suitable type of wine for your guests; how much wine to buy; how to serve it effortlessly; and, finally – how to survive hangovers.

WHAT'S THE OCCASION?

A big, one-off celebration – a wedding reception, a christening, or a special birthday – calls for the best wine you can afford. We look at serving wine at formal occasions in more detail on page 142.

■ If people are sitting down to a meal, match the wine to the food (see pages 46–7).

■ If you are planning a drinks party, either with canapés or a more substantial buffet, keep it simple by serving only one or two choices of wine.

The time of year

The season and outdoor temperature should be considered when choosing wine. For summer parties or barbecues, keep the wine light and cool. A Chardonnay or Sancerre will both be popular choices – make sure they are well-chilled. Have sparkling mineral or soda water on hand, so that people can make Spritzers (see page 154). You can serve red wine – but pick one with little or no oak. Try a light Merlot, Pinot Noir or rosé, and chill beforehand.

If you are choosing wine for a more formal picnic, such as a special racing event, or an evening of opera or outdoor theatre, the most popular choice is good-quality Champagne.

In the winter, almost anything goes, but keep heavy red wine for dinner. If serving only canapés, try Champagne, or a hot wine drink (see page 151).

Glasses

The shape of the glass is a secondary consideration at most parties. For sparkling wine, you'll want flutes, but for serving still wine, any basic shape is fine. Glasses can be hired from most wine stores, but check if the glasses are clean beforehand, as the last thing you want is to discover dirty glasses just as your guests arrive.

party planner tips

■ Set up a bar table away from where the food will be served, to provide easy access for the guests. The kitchen is ideal, so you can clean spills easily.

■ If your refrigerator is too small to keep wine cool, buy bags of ice and fill the bath with ice and water for an impromptu large ice bucket.

■ Everybody will expect a drink when they arrive. Have some of the bottles opened, and the corks put back halfway in, before the first guest is due to arrive. This prevents accidental spills, and makes the corks easy to pull out when guests appear.

■ Remember to have plenty of water on offer. If any of your guests don't drink alcohol, you may want to get in a supply of their favourite soft drink.

Working with your budget

How much should you buy? When you have calculated how many bottles you need (see above), work out how much you can afford to pay per bottle.

Discounts Ask for a discount for any quantities over 12 bottles. If you see wine that is discounted, ask why. It could be that a new vintage is about to be released, and you may choose to wait for the fresher wine.

Finding a bargain Wine stores have sales like all other stores, so it is worth waiting for sale time, if you are buying in bulk. Sparkling wine and Champagne are often discounted before and after Christmas.

LOW-ALCOHOL WINE

No-alcohol wine has had its alcohol removed; low-alcohol wine has been partially fermented. Providing a no- or low-alcohol wine for guests is a good idea – the white wines seem to be more successful than the red, though it may be more cost-effective to make Spritzers.

AVOIDING HANGOVERS

The ill-effects (headache, nausea, dizziness and vomiting) we call a hangover are caused primarily by dehydration. Adhering to moderate consumption levels (see above) will help to minimize these effects, as will eating and drinking plenty of water. To reduce the chances of getting a hangover:

The night before...
- *Eat properly before and during drinking. Avoid very rich foods which might aggravate your stomach.*
- *Drink plenty of water – ideally, have a glass of water for every glass of wine you drink.*
- *Choose or make Spritzers or Coolers (see page 154).*

The morning after...
- *Drink plenty of water to counter the effects of dehydration. Avoid drinks containing caffeine, which will dehydrate you even further.*
- *Eat breakfast to boost your glucose levels. Dishes containing eggs are a good choice as they contain cysteine, which aids the body's detoxification.*

Chardonnay, Chablis and White Burgundy

Chardonnay wines are very easy to match with food. They go well with both meat and fish, although you should avoid serving them with very oily food. Excellent Chablis and other white Burgundies suit a variety of seafood and white meat dishes.

WE RECOMMEND	
White fish and seafood	● ● ● ● ●
White meat	● ● ● ● ●
Canapés	● ● ● ●
Pasta	● ● ●
Vegetarian dishes	● ● ●

Chardonnay

Rich, oaked Chardonnay is wonderful with Mediterranean-influenced cuisine. Marinaded and grilled pork, tuna and chicken served with peppers and a dash of chilli, will all work well.

Alternatively, serve a good Chardonnay with delicious bread, salami, green olives and couscous for a relaxed, easy lunch. Pan-fried monkfish would also be good.

Chablis

Traditional Chablis has a wonderful steely, mineral flavour which makes it an ideal companion for roast chicken, fish and vegetarian dishes. Oysters, seafood risotto, grilled shrimp, pan-fried salmon and grilled or boiled lobster all do justice to an excellent Chablis. A mature, oaked Chablis would be best served with a meaty fish such as swordfish or tuna.

White Burgundy

The term "white Burgundy" covers a wide range of wines including Mâcon and Côte de Beaune. Full-bodied and nutty, a special occasion white Burgundy should be served with roast chicken, garlic shrimps, grilled salmon or lobster.

Truffle oil sprinkled over some mashed potato and served with excellent pork sausages would make a delicious bistro-style meal. Rich mushroom risottos are also good with white Burgundy.

148

BRAISED LOBSTER WITH TOMATO CONFIT

This elegant seafood dish is just right for excellent Chardonnay or white Burgundy.

SERVES 2

1 bay leaf
1 sprig of thyme
1 lobster (about 1 kg/2 lb)
50 ml (2 fl oz) olive oil
1 tsp tomato purée
100 ml (4 fl oz) white wine
50 ml (2 fl oz) brandy
1 litre (40 fl oz/2 pints) fish stock
200 ml (7 fl oz/¹⁄₃ pint) crème fraîche
1 small shallot, finely chopped
1 small clove garlic, finely chopped
*4 plum tomatoes, peeled, deseeded
  and quartered*
2 sprigs of basil, to garnish
salt and pepper, to taste

Bring a large pan of water to the boil and add the bay leaf and thyme. Boil the lobster for 8–10 minutes, then remove and leave to cool. Shell the lobster tail and claws, discarding the head and innards.

Sauté the lobster shells in 2 teaspoons of the olive oil. Add the tomato purée, white wine and brandy and simmer until reduced by half. Add the fish stock and simmer until about a quarter remains. Strain the sauce, and add the crème fraîche. Simmer gently for 2–3 minutes, and season.

To make the tomato confit, heat the remaining olive oil in a pan and add the shallots, garlic and tomato quarters. Cover, and cook gently for 15 minutes.

To serve, divide the confit between two plates. Slice the lobster tail into medallions and remove the claw from the shell. Place the lobster pieces on the confit, and drizzle with the crème fraîche sauce. Garnish each plate with a sprig of basil.

149

Red Wine DRINKS

Red wine is used in a wide range of mixed drinks, including the classic Spanish drink, Sangría, and the hot punches Glühwein and Mulled Wine. The most versatile wine in terms of temperature, red wine works well with many other ingredients, and can be served ice cold, at room temperature, warm or hot.

VERSATILE RED WINE

We tend not to serve red wine on warm days, but it can be delicious served cold. You could make a Spritzer (see right), or serve sparkling red wine. It should, like all sparkling wine, be served ice-cold. Use good quality light red wine for making a chilled drink, and consider using a sparkling red wine. When heating red wine, choose a full-bodied red that will complement the addition of fruit and spices. Spicing red wine disguises its faults, and will improve the flavour of an average wine.

PEEL TWISTS

Use to garnish any red or white wine mixed drink. To make, use a canelle knife to pare away a single fine strip of peel, spiralling carefully down from the top of the fruit to the bottom. Aim for strips at least 5 cm (2 in) long.

CLOVE-STUDDED LEMON SLICES

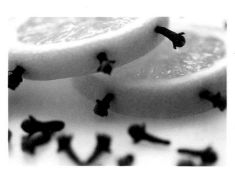

1 Cut off both ends of a lemon and discard the ends. Hold the lemon firmly and cut into slices about ½ cm (¼ in) thick, using a gentle sawing action.

2 Place each slice flat on the chopping board, and firmly press cloves into the peel, approximately 1½ cm (¾ in) apart, working around the slice.

RED WINE SPRITZER You can use any light-bodied red wine for a Spritzer. This is a great way to serve red wine in the summer. Pour a glass of red wine over two or three ice cubes in a highball glass, and top with soda water or sparkling mineral water.

MULLED WINE

SERVES 6

125 ml caster sugar

1 cinnamon stick

6 clove-studded lemon slices

(see below left)

125 ml water

1 x 75 cl bottle red wine

Heat the sugar, cinnamon stick and lemon slices in the water, and before it reaches boiling point, turn off the heat and let stand for 30 minutes.

Strain the spiced water and return to the pan. Add the wine and stir until well mixed. Heat again slowly until just before boiling point, stirring gently, then remove from the heat to serve.

SANGRÍA

SERVES 6

1 tray ice cubes

125 ml orange juice

100 g caster sugar

500 ml sparkling lemonade

60 ml brandy

1 x 75 cl bottle red wine

2 oranges or lemons, sliced

Place the ice in a punch bowl or pitcher, then pour over the orange juice and sugar. Stir thoroughly until the sugar is dissolved.

Add the lemonade, brandy and red wine, and mix them well using either a punch ladle or a wooden spoon. Add the orange or lemon slices before serving.

bartender tips

■ When heating wine, do not allow it to boil, as this will ruin the flavour of the wine.

■ When serving drinks from a punch bowl, use a ladle – never dip cups or glasses into the liquid as they may break, leaving shards of glass in your punch.

■ If serving hot drinks, ensure your ladle and cups or glasses are heatsafe and have handles. Take care not to overfill the cups or glasses as you may accidentally spill the hot liquid on the person holding the cup.

Food with

Sancerre, Pouilly-Fumé and Sauvignon Blanc

All of the Sauvignon Blanc wines have a reputation for being excellent wines to serve with seafood because of their herbaceous flavours and lingering length. These wines are good with light, delicately flavoured dishes and mild cheeses.

WE RECOMMEND	
Fish and shellfish	● ● ● ● ●
Canapés	● ● ● ● ●
Cheese	● ● ● ●
Egg	● ● ●
Vegetarian dishes	● ● ●

Sancerre

A young Sancerre can be rather acidic, but this edge works beautifully with canapés and tapas dishes such as grilled squid, cuttlefish and tortilla. All fish and shellfish are a good accompaniment for Sancerre. Salmon is good for special occasions – serve it with a little lemon juice or topped with Dijon mustard.

The slightly gooseberry notes of Sancerre also marry well with the sharp flavour and the dry texture of goat's cheese.

Pouilly-Fumé

The distinctive smokiness of these crisp and concentrated dry whites means that they are a very successful match with shellfish. Medallions of lobster tossed in butter and lemon or crab meat in a creamy sauce are excellent options.

Like Sancerre, Pouilly-Fumé is an excellent choice when you are serving canapés. To show off a well-chilled Pouilly-Fumé, serve smoked salmon or chicken liver pâté on crostini.

Sauvignon Blanc

The Sauvignon Blanc wines of the New World are excellent food wines because of their lifted, herby aromas, their tropical flavours on the palate and their good length.

You can serve almost any fish or vegetarian dish with Sauvignon Blanc, but an ideal choice is asparagus with hollandaise sauce – the crispness of the wine cuts through the creamy sauce.

SALMON PARCELS AND FONDANT POTATOES

The delicate flavour of salmon cooked with flaky pastry teases the palate and allows the flavours of these pungent dry white wines to develop fully.

SERVES 4

6 sheets filo pastry
100 g (4 oz) butter, melted
4 salmon fillets, skinned
  and boned
salt and pepper, to taste
4 small waxy potatoes,
  cut into round shapes
50 g (2 oz) butter
50 ml (2 fl oz) olive oil
125 ml (4 fl oz) vegetable stock
4 cherry tomatoes, deep-fried whole
chives and chervil, to garnish
4 plum tomatoes, peeled and
  chopped, to garnish (optional)

Preheat the oven to 220°C (425°F/gas 7).

Brush one sheet of pastry with some of the melted butter, place another layer on top, brush with butter and repeat with a third layer. Cut in half and repeat with the remaining three sheets – to produce four squares.

Place the squares on a baking sheet. Season the salmon fillets and place one in the centre of each filo square. Fold the edges over the salmon to form a parcel. Seal the edges and brush with melted butter. Bake for about 15 minutes until crisp and golden brown. Remove and turn down the oven temperature to 180°C (350°F/gas 4).

For the fondant potato, fry the potato in the butter and oil until golden, add the stock and transfer to the oven until tender, for about 15 minutes.

To serve, arrange the salmon parcels and potatoes as shown. Place a cherry tomato on top of each potato and garnish with chives and chervil. You could also lay some chopped tomato around the edge.

153

WHITE *Wine* DRINKS

Mixed wine drinks are an excellent option for parties, particularly if budget is a factor. They are festive and can provide a lighter alternative to wine whenever you fancy a change. Here we look at some of the classic white wine drinks, along with suggestions on how to add the finishing touches for party versions.

IN THE MIX

White wine can be used to make a variety of delicious drinks. The three classic drinks are Coolers, Spritzers and Kirs. To make a Cooler, pour a glass of dry white wine over ice in a highball glass and top with lemonade. To make a Spritzer, use sparkling mineral or soda water instead. To make Kir, add a dash of crème de cassis to a glass of white wine. White wine is also very good as the base for a fruit punch (see right).

There is even a hot mulled white wine drink – white glögg – an essential element of the Swedish Christmas season. Try the recipe for Glühwein on page 151, replacing the red wine with white.

For most white wine drinks, however, the wine is served ice-cold. Do not use your best wine for ice-cold drinks as you cannot taste the full range of flavour – don't, however, use a poor-quality wine that you wouldn't normally buy. A dry wine such as Chardonnay or Semillon would be ideal.

Stay chilled

For best results, all the ingredients in a cold wine drink should be thoroughly chilled, and only removed from the refrigerator moments before use. Drinks served in tall glasses should contain two or three ice cubes – don't be tempted to use more as they will dilute the drink. Do not use ice in drinks containing sparkling wine, as the wine will lose its carbonation.

For large quantities of a mixed drink, such as punch, use a whole block of ice rather than cubes. The smaller total surface area reduces the melting time of the ice, keeping the drink colder for longer.

- *Make an ice block or ring by filling a plastic container or ring mould with water and freezing.*
- *Don't use crushed ice, as it will dilute the drink quickly.*

CITRUS FRUIT WEDGES

Use lemon or lime wedges to garnish a Spritzer or Cooler. Hold the fruit on one side and cut away thin strips of peel using a canelle knife, moving around the fruit so the pith is revealed in bands. Cut the fruit into six wedges.

HERB OR FRUIT ICE CUBES

1 Fill the compartments of an ice cube tray a third full of water and freeze for 2–3 hours until firm.

2 Place a herb leaf, berry or small pieces of fruit in each section, add another third of cold water and freeze. Then top-up and freeze once more. Add to Coolers and Spritzers in place of regular ice cubes for a special touch.

what's in a name?

Cocktail The earliest definition of "cocktail" to appear in print was in the periodical *The Balance* in 1806: "Cocktail is a stimulating liquor, composed of spirits of any kind, sugar, water and bitters". Many countries have a tradition of serving mixed drinks, which makes it difficult to trace the origin of the word.

Stirrers

By using a stirrer (or swizzle-stick), you can make sure that the ingredients in your white wine drinks are evenly distributed. There are many designs available that will do the job. Choose a type that reaches the bottom of your chosen glass, is flexible and strong, will not break or splinter and can be washed and re-used. The bubbles in sparkling wine drinks will, however, mix the ingredients themselves and may lose their carbonation if stirred.

WHITE WINE PUNCH

SERVES 20

block of ice to fit your punch bowl
3 x 75 cl bottles dry white wine (you could replace some of the wine with fruit juice, if you prefer)
375 ml (13 fl oz) liqueur, of your choice
450 g (1 lb) seasonal fruit, sliced
a few sprigs of borage or mint

Place the block of ice in the base of a large punch bowl. Pour over the wine and liqueur, and stir gently using a wooden spoon or punch ladle.

Just before serving, add the fruit and stir gently, until the fruit is evenly distributed across the surface. Scatter the sprigs of borage or mint over the surface to garnish.

SPARKLING WHITE WINE AND

Champagne

DRINKS

The most famous sparkling white wine is Champagne from the eponymous region of France, but there are fine sparkling wines produced in other parts of the world, which, according to European law, are not allowed to use the name. You can use either to make delicious mixed drinks – perfect for parties and celebrations.

SPARKLING WINE COCKTAILS

Where the terms Champagne or sparkling wine are used in recipes, the two can be used interchangeably, according to your taste and budget. Spanish Cava, Italian Prosecco and German Sekt are all delicious sparkling white wines, perfect for mixing with other ingredients to create tasty celebratory cocktails. You can also use sparkling red wine as a mixer – the same techniques apply.

Champagne cocktails

One in five bottles of Champagne consumed in France is used for cocktails. Although it is rarely worth using a super-premium bottle of Champagne, using a good-quality Champagne that you would buy for drinking on its own will ensure that you enjoy your cocktail. In the earliest days of Champagne production it was often flavoured with sugar and bitters. This flavouring is still popular today in the form of the classic Champagne Cocktail (see opposite).

Sparkling wine and champagne cocktails are rarely shaken or stirred, as the movement of the bubbles will mix the ingredients. Additional agitation will cause the wine to lose its sparkle (*mousse*).

FROSTING A GLASS

1 Pour sugar syrup or liqueur onto a saucer to cover the bottom thinly. Pour a generous amount of caster sugar onto a second saucer and gently shake the plate from side to side until the sugar is spread out flat.

2 Ensure that your glass is clean and dry, then lightly dip the rim into the first saucer. Shake gently, then dip the rim into the second saucer.

BITTERSWEET *A white sugar cube flavoured with two drops of Angostura bitters will add flavour to the drink and enhance the mousse.*

THE CHAMPAGNE COCKTAIL

1 sugar cube, flavoured with
  Angostura bitters (see left)
150 ml (5 fl oz/¼ pint) Champagne
1 lemon peel twist (see page 150)

Place the flavoured sugar cube into the bottom of a Champagne flute.

Slightly tilt the glass, and add the Champagne. When the Champagne has settled, drop in the lemon peel twist.

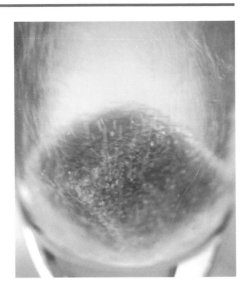

BLACK VELVET

Draft Guinness
Champagne

Carefully pour Guinness into a flute until the glass is about half full. Leave the Guinness to settle for 1–2 minutes.

Slowly add the Champagne, filling to within ½ cm (¼ in) of the rim. Gently stir with a tall spoon or stirrer.

BELLINI

50 ml (2 fl oz) puréed white peaches
1 tsp crème de pêche (peach liqueur)
75 ml (2½ fl oz) Champagne or Prosecco

Carefully pour the peach purée into a glass. Add the crème de pêche and stir very gently.

Slightly tilt the glass, and gently add the Champagne or Prosecco, filling to within ½ cm (¼ in) of the rim.

Natural partners

- - - - - - - - - - - - - - - - - - - -

Fruit juice, purée, liqueur, brandy or schnapps will blend well with sparkling wine or Champagne if used in appropriate quantities:

■ **75 ml (2½ fl oz)**:	50 ml juice or purée
■ **125 ml (4 fl oz)**:	25 ml liqueur, brandy or schnapps

The classic combinations are orange juice (for a Buck's fizz) and peach purée (for a Bellini), but almost any juicy fruit will taste delicious with sparkling wine or Champagne.

Riesling

This elegant wine varies according to where it is produced, but it is safe to say that most Rieslings taste clean, crisp and fragrant. They leave the palate cleansed and refreshed, particularly at dessert time, but can be served successfully with a wide variety of foods.

WE RECOMMEND	
Fish and seafood	•••••
White meat	•••••
Red meat	•••
Pasta	•••
Fruit desserts	•••

Old World

The Rieslings of Germany and France are characteristically light and aromatic and can range from dry to sweet. They are best served with simply cooked food, such as stir-fried or poached dishes.

Young, fresh Rieslings are perfect with seafood – particularly oysters or scallops with a hint of freshly squeezed lemon juice and a little freshly ground black pepper. Serve with a mixed leaf and flower salad to achieve a very special combination of flavours.

Older Rieslings develop into rich, buttery, complex wines. To enhance a special older Riesling, serve it with a traditional French veal ragoût flavoured with tomato on buttered noodles.

Poultry can work beautifully with German Spätlese or Auslese or French late harvest wines. Goose or duck, poached and served with a simple fruit sauce, will be brought to life by these sweeter wines.

Riesling's freshness and lightness make it an ideal partner for a sweet conclusion to a meal. Fruit-based desserts – particularly apple- or peach-based – are perfect.

New World

Australian Rieslings are richer than those of the Old World and have fuller, fruitier flavours. They can have a slightly toasty undertone, too, which makes them a great match for fish pâtés, cold white meats and roast vegetable dishes. The New World wines can also stand up to some of the milder curries, but be careful not to overpower the subtler flavours in the wine.

New Zealand produces Rieslings that are closer to the German style, but they also produce some very sweet dessert wines that can be drunk very young and are a great match with most fruity desserts.

ROAST PEACHES WITH VANILLA SYRUP

Fruit-based desserts, such as these succulent peaches, benefit from Riesling's freshness and lightness.

SERVES 4

2 *ripe peaches, pitted and quartered*
2 *ripe nectarines, pitted and*
   quartered
100 g (3½ oz) *demerara sugar*
50 g (2 oz) *butter*
100 g (3½ oz) *caster sugar*
100 ml (4 fl oz) *water*
4 *mint sprigs, to garnish*
2 *vanilla pods, halved*
8 *star anise*
100 g (3½ oz) *dark brown sugar*
1 *tbsp balsamic vinegar*

Preheat the oven to 220˚C (425˚F/gas 7).

Place the peach and nectarine quarters, skin side down, onto a large piece of foil. Sprinkle the fruit with the demerara sugar, and place a little butter onto each fruit quarter. Seal the edges of the foil together to make a parcel and place onto a baking tray. Bake for 15 minutes, or until the fruit is tinged golden brown.

Heat the caster sugar with the water, and add the seeds from the vanilla pods and the star anise. Bring to the boil and simmer gently until reduced.

In a separate pan, heat the dark brown sugar over a low heat until melted and golden caramel in colour. Remove from the heat and add a tablespoon of water.

To serve, divide the fruit between four plates. Pour the vanilla syrup over the fruit and drizzle the caramel syrup and the balsamic vinegar around the plates as shown.

159

Many centuries ago, all wine was transported in casks and was vulnerable to spoilage and oxidation. Producers fortified the wine by adding high-alcohol grape spirit to stabilize the wine. Sherry, port, Madeira, Marsala and brandy (strictly a pure grape spirit) are the most popular fortified wines, and make excellent alternatives for the wine enthusiast.

This chapter introduces each type of wine, explaining their different origins, how they are made, and which are considered the best of each type – particularly with a view to investment. Fortified wines are occasional drinks, so we discuss how to store them so that they retain their quality over time. The chapter also looks at how and when to serve them for maximum enjoyment.

fortified
wine and grape spirits

Sherry

One of the most popular apéritifs in the world, sherry is fortified wine made from white grapes. There are two main types of sherry – fino and oloroso – and here we explain how sherry is made, how each type assumes its distinct character and how to store and serve sherry to ensure you enjoy it at its very best.

HOW SHERRY IS MADE

Sherry originates from three towns in Andalucía, Spain – Jerez de la Frontera (the word sherry is derived from "Jerez"), Puerto de Santa Maria and Sanlúcar. It is also made elsewhere in Spain, Cyprus, Australia and California, but in the 1990s, after much effort on the part of the Jerez producers, the sherry industry agreed to restrict the use of the word sherry to describe only the produce of the Jerez region.

The sherry-making process begins when a white wine is produced from the local grape variety, palomino. The wine is then fortified – alcohol is added – and the alcoholic strength determines the type of sherry. Fino-type sherries contain about 15 per cent alcohol, whereas olorosos are strengthened to around 18 per cent.

Over the next two to three months, the wine will develop in one of two ways. In the more

KEEP IT SHORT Use any tulip-shaped glass for sherry. Fill to no more than one-third full, to appreciate the aroma.

serving sherry

- Freshness is of primary importance when buying fino. Buy from outlets such as supermarkets where the turnover is constant. Once the bottle has been opened, it should be kept in a refrigerator and drunk within three days. Fino should be served very cold. The ideal glass is a tall, thin "copita", but you could use a small tulip-shaped glass. Delicious served with shellfish, such as freshly cooked shrimp.
- Oloroso and amontillado will last for 2–3 weeks after you have opened the bottle, but will start to deteriorate after this time. They are ideal as winter apéritifs – warming and nutty. Serve them in a glass that tapers a little towards the top so that you focus the aromas. These sherries complement soups, especially consommés, or you can enjoy them with nuts as an apéritif or following a meal.
- Cream sherries will keep for 2–3 months after opening. There is no need to refrigerate. Serve in a tapered sherry glass. Good cream sherries are delicious on their own, but you could serve them poured over high-quality vanilla ice cream.

FINE FINO The famous Gonzalez Byass Tío Pepe estate, in Jerez, Andalucía, produces very high quality fino sherries using traditional methods.

delicate, less alcoholic fino barrels, a yeast known as "flor" settles on the wine, which imparts a tangy, yeast flavour. The flor develops slowly into a layer covering the surface of the wine and prevents it from oxidizing any further, so the resultant sherry is pale and light.

The higher alcoholic content of oloroso wine inhibits the growth of the flor, so the wine ages in contact with the air. Oloroso sherries are thus darker and richer than fino sherries.

The origins of flor are a mystery, but it is very common in Jerez and virtually nonexistent elsewhere. This is why the sherry from the Jerez region is considered to be the most authentic.

The solera system

The sherry producers have a system of barrel-ageing, called the "solera" system, which is a crucial part of the production process. The solera barrels are topped-up with new wine as the mature sherry is bottled, to ensure that the wine ages evenly and that the quality of the sherry produced remains consistent. The sherry casks are kept in bodegas (barrel stores), which encourages some of the wine to evaporate and results in further fortification – some old oloroso sherries have an alcohol content of up to 24 per cent.

sherry styles

Fino Pale, dry sherry. Light body and the most delicate flavour of all the sherries. Finos are fragrant, refreshing and tangy, and can be very good value.

Manzanilla Very dry fino-style sherry made only in Sanlúcar. Said to contain a slight flavour of salt as a result of Sanlúcar's proximity to the sea. Another Sanlúcar specialty is an aged manzanilla known as manzanilla pasada. Both are zesty and fresh, and make good apéritifs.

Amontillado A fino that has aged to develop a fuller flavour. An authentic amontillado is dry, nutty and concentrated, not unlike an oloroso – although often more elegant. True, unblended amontillado is difficult to find. It is often sweetened to be sold under a medium or medium-dry label.

Oloroso Rich and nutty in flavour, olorosos are aged for years (sometimes up to 100 years). The best olorosos are dry, whereas mass-produced olorosos are quite often sweetened. Some very old olorosos are too austere to be enjoyed in their natural dry state, and need to be lightly sweetened to be drinkable. Thus styles of even top-quality olorosos can vary.

Palo cortado Made from the wine that has not developed sufficient flor to make a fino and mature along the same lines as a lighter-bodied oloroso. Styles vary from producer to producer.

Cream These are sweet blends of sherry, often of inferior quality, as the top sherries will be sold as finos and olorosos. Some cream sherries are delicious, but in general, this is the sector of sherry production that has most contributed to sherry's poor image.

PX There are a few sherries made from a variety of grapes called Pedro Ximénez. These are sun-dried grapes (essentially raisins) and the result is a very sweet treacly wine, almost black in colour, entirely different from classic sherry. Its principal use is as a blending wine for oloroso, amontillado and cream sherry.

Gewürztraminer, Pinot Gris and Sylvaner

Spicy, floral and scented, these famous wines from Alsace, near the German border in France, were made to complement the diverse foods of this region. Serve with a typical Alsace dish, such as onion flan, or try a fillet of creamy trout.

Gewürztraminer

Pinot Gris

Sylvaner

The tell-tale spiciness that defines Gewürztraminer is a great partner for delicately spiced foods, but the secret is to get the balance right. A Thai salad with prawns, mint, lime and shallots makes a superb combination, but be careful not to overpower with chilli.

Roasted pork served with apple sauce, roast onions, garlic and braised cabbage would be a more traditional choice.

The high acidity of Pinot Gris sets it apart from Gewürztraminer. It still has the spiciness to stand up to spicy foods, however, and it works well with some white meats. It would also suit a selection of meat and fish canapés.

Pinot Gris is good with vegetable dishes, such as courgette or onion flan. Lightly poached pears with cinnamon would be a good match with one of the richer Pinot Gris.

This is at its best in its youth. It is perfumed and has a slight bitterness and high acidity. As such, it is a pleasant accompaniment to many fish and chicken dishes, particularly those in cream-based sauces. Serve with a small amount of fruit to pick up the fruit flavours of the wine.

Braised sausage and pork dishes flavoured with citrus fruit are good with Sylvaner – the fruit's acidity suits the acidity of the wine.

PAN-FRIED TROUT FILLETS WITH GRAPES AND A CHIVE BUTTER SAUCE

The creamy texture of fish in sauce makes a wonderful contrast to the spicy acidity of most Alsace wines.

SERVES 2

650 g (1 lb 7 oz) small waxy potatoes
25 ml (1 fl oz) olive oil
2 trout fillets, trimmed, and all fine
    bones removed
25 g (1 oz) butter
25 ml (1 fl oz) vegetable oil
200 g (7 oz) green seedless grapes
2 shallots, finely sliced
25 ml (1 oz) white wine vinegar
25 ml (1 oz) white wine
80 ml (3 fl oz) double cream
300 g (10 oz) cold butter, diced
1 tomato, peeled, deseeded and diced
2 tbsp finely chopped chives

Peel, then boil the potatoes in salted water for 15 minutes or until cooked. Drain and mash with the olive oil.

Meanwhile, pan fry the fillets in the butter and oil, until golden (about 2 minutes on each side). Remove from the pan, and leave to rest. Add the grapes to the pan and fry until tinged golden brown.

In a separate pan, place the shallots, white wine vinegar and white wine and simmer until reduced. Add the cream and reduce by about half, then gradually whisk in the butter. Strain through a fine sieve.

To serve, place a large oval of mashed potato on the centre of each plate and lay the trout fillet over the top. Arrange a circle of grapes around the plate. Scatter the tomato and chives around the trout and pour over the sauce as shown.

165

Port

Port is made by adding brandy to partially fermented red wine. It is produced from vineyards located around the River Douro in northern Portugal. Only since the 18th century has port been fortified, probably to preserve it for export. The style is much imitated, with port-style wines produced in Australia, South Africa, California and elsewhere.

AN INTRODUCTION TO PORT

Almost 100 000 acres are devoted to the production of port, and there are considerable climatic differences between the regions. In addition, over 80 grape varieties are planted. As a result, there are many styles of port produced, and the quality varies greatly. Broadly speaking, the best ports come from the hotter, drier, more easterly vineyards.

A few port houses still tread the grapes by foot, although most have introduced mechanised treading. Any unsavoury associations with feet can be dismissed: the high alcohol content of the finished wine will kill off any bacteria. Fermentation takes place in tanks especially designed to extract colour, tannin and other compounds as rapidly as possible. While there is still ample residual sugar in the wine, the fermentation is arrested by the addition of grape brandy. This has the effect of raising the alcohol level to around 20 per cent, while conserving a good deal of sweetness in the wine.

PORT STYLES

The great majority of ports are non-vintage – that is, they are blended from wine produced over several years. The most basic style of port is ruby, usually a three-year-old wine with no great complexity.

Tawny port

Commercial tawny port is made by blending red and white ports, but top-quality tawnies – such as 10 and 20 year olds – are blends of older red wines which are aged for long periods in casks. The long ageing period moderates the tannins and brings out a wonderful complexity of flavour. A good tawny port has nuances of figs, caramel, honey and dried fruits.

PORT COLOUR *Port comes in a variety of colours, echoing the different blends and varying ageing processes. Vintage and LBV ports are reddish; tawnies are amber or brown.*

166

Ruby and white port

These tend to be inexpensive blends intended to preserve fruit in the wine. Ruby port is made from red grapes and white port is made from white grapes. White is less sweet than ruby, and both are popular as an apéritif, or served with cheese after a meal.

Late bottled vintage (LBV) port

A blended port that is given longer cask-ageing than basic ruby and white port – between four and six years – before being bottled. At under half the price of vintage port, these LBVs can be bargains, although styles and qualities often vary considerably from shipper to shipper.

Vintage port

Always made from the best and ripest grapes, vintage port is made from a single grape variety, and aged for at least two years. Not every vintage will be "declared" as a vintage port year; in theory, only the outstanding years are declared, which occurs only three to four times a decade. Vintage port will need ageing in the bottle for at least 15 years to develop its full potential. By the time it is ready to drink it will have a sediment and will need decanting (see pages 128–9).

A single quinta vintage port comes from a single estate (quinta), and is usually produced only in years when there hasn't been a vintage declaration.

BUYING PORT

Port is fairly indestructible, so ruby, tawny and vintage ports can safely be bought from supermarkets, as well as individual wine merchants. For older vintages, you should contact established wine merchants. Auction houses are also a good source of old vintage ports, sometimes at surprisingly reasonable prices. Vintage port is bottled in dark heavy glass and often sealed with wax, so oxidation and leakages are very rare. Store the bottles on their sides.

LYING IN WAIT These densely packed bottles of port are destined to age for several years. They will lie on their sides undisturbed for years or even decades.

Port tongs

These are sometimes used to open bottles of vintage port whose corks are stuck fast. Heat the tongs in an open fire until they are red hot and apply them to the neck of the bottle – make sure that the bottle is standing upright. The sudden heat cracks the glass and the top of the bottle – cork and all – comes off cleanly.

serving port

■ Many ports – rubies, all tawnies, white port and young LBVs – do not need to be decanted and should be poured straight from the bottle. Vintage port, however, does need decanting to separate the wine from the gritty deposit (see pages 128–9).

■ Serve all types of port in medium-sized tapered glasses.
■ Tawny ports make a delicious after-dinner drink. Serve with light desserts. A few young tawnies can be lightly chilled.
■ Rubies, whites and LBVs can generally be kept for up to a week after the bottle

has been opened. White port should always be served chilled.
■ Vintage ports are the classic after-dinner drink. For maximum enjoyment, they should be consumed within 2–3 days of decanting.

Madeira AND Marsala

These two great wines are not as fashionable for drinking today as they once were. Both are made in many different styles, which can be confusing, and many poor quality Madeiras and Marsalas have been produced, damaging their images. Both are often called for in recipes, but it would be good to see them restored to their former popularity.

MADEIRA

The island of Madeira was planted with vines by its Portuguese conquerors in the 15th century. The great age of Madeira was the 18th and 19th centuries, when the wine had a huge following in Europe and the USA. Unfortunately, a vine-destroying louse known as phylloxera wiped out a great many of Madeira's vineyards, and Madeira began to lose its popularity. The most authentic Madeira is that produced from the so-called "noble" grape varieties:

serving madeira

- Choose a tapered glass similar to a port glass.
- Decanting is not necessary, but it should be left to breathe before serving (see pages 128–9).
- Serve Sercial and Verdelho lightly chilled as apéritif wines, but Bual and Malmsey should be served at room temperature. Madeira is delicious served with soups, and with most desserts.
- It is a robust wine and will last almost indefinitely.

Sercial The sercial grapes are difficult to grow, have high acidity and produce the driest style of Madeira wine.

Verdelho A medium-dry style with more body but less richness than Sercial. It has a smoky complexity and an invigorating tanginess.

Bual Known as Boal in Portuguese, this is medium-sweet to sweet Madeira. It is often the fruitiest of all Madeiras and is opulent, but without excessive richness.

Malmsey The sweetest Madeira. Made from the malvasia grape, it is honeyed and lush, with overtones of figs and chocolate. Very heady, strong and rich. Not cloying, as the sweetness is balanced by acidity.

All other Madeira is made from the grape variety tinta negra mole and is often labelled as dry, medium dry, medium sweet and sweet. EU regulations state that a wine named after a particular variety of grape must contain at least 85 per cent of wine made from that grape. Before 1993, some Madeira producers used the names of the noble varieties for their products, which were often inferior and often totally unrelated. This has also contributed to the decline in popularity of Madeira as a drink.

CHILLED OR WARMED *Each style of Madeira suits a different serving temperature, to bring out its flavours.*

madeira styles

Generic wine Made from tinta negra mole. Aged for 18 months. Often coloured and sweetened with caramel. Use only for cooking.

Finest Made from tinta negra mole. Aged for 3 years.

5 year Made from tinta negra mole.

10 year Made from a noble grape variety.

15 year Made from a noble grape variety. Quite rare, usually very high quality.

Solera Made in a solera barrel system. An increasingly rare style, but look out for 19th-century Soleras at auction.

Vintage Made from a noble grape variety. Aged for at least 20 years.

marsala styles

Fine Aged for less than 1 year.

Superiore Aged for at least 2 years.

Riserva Aged for at least 4 years.

Vergine Aged for at least 5 years.

Stravecchio or Riserva Aged for at least 10 years.

Secco/Semisecco Dry/Semi-dry.

Dolce Sweet.

Madeira at its best

The top of the range is vintage Madeira, which must be aged in cask for at least 20 years. Most shippers hold stocks of very old wines that are still for sale (at a high price) and such wines, often dating back to the 19th century or earlier, also turn up regularly at wine auctions. They can be excellent value for wines of such an age, and are often outstanding.

MARSALA

This fortified wine from Sicily first found international favour in the 1770s, when it began to be exported to Britain where it enjoyed great popularity. Made from the local grape varieties, Marsala is made in a similar way to sherry, often in a solera system (see page 163).

Whereas Madeira styles are based on noble grape varieties or degrees of sweetness, Marsala is categorised according to colour, age and sweetness. Most labels will describe all three.

Marsala is widely used for cooking but it is regaining some of its popularity as an apéritif. Regulations dating from 1984 have seen the end of the flavoured Marsalas – often with added egg yolk or coffee – that did so much damage to the image of the wine.

Marsala at its best

The premium Marsalas are "Superiore" and "Vergine", aged for two and five years respectively; Vergine Riserva or Stravecchio wines are at least ten years old. The most distinctive of Marsalas, and

some would say the best, are made by Marco De Bartoli, who insists on picking grapes so ripe that he considers fortification unnecessary. His range of 10-, 20- and 30-year-old Marsalas are called Vecchio Samperi, and are unfortified and unsweetened. The Marsalas produced by Pellegrino and Florio are also of outstanding quality.

AGEING IN THE BARREL Vintage Madeira is aged for at least twenty years in large oak barrels.

serving marsala

■ Serve in a tapered wine glass, such as a port glass.
■ There is no need to decant Marsala.
■ The drier the style, the cooler the temperature at which Marsala should be served. On a warm evening, it would be more appropriate to serve even a sweet Marsala lightly chilled.
■ Marsala is delicious served as an apéritif, or as an after-dinner drink.
■ It will last for 2–3 months after opening.

Sauternes and Muscat

Rich and luscious, but with a dry clean finish, these sweet wines are a delicious way to start or end a meal. You can serve them with a savoury starter or a rich dessert – they will enhance the key flavours and textures to give a taste sensation.

WE RECOMMEND	
Fruit desserts	● ● ● ● ●
Chocolate desserts	● ● ● ●
Ginger desserts	● ● ● ●
Cheese	● ● ● ●
Meat pâté	● ● ● ●

Sauternes

It is the richness and glycerin-like texture of this sweet wine that makes it so versatile and compatible with such a diversity of foods. Traditionally, Sauternes is served with foie gras. The marriage of creaminess and mouthfeel brings out the best in both the food and the wine. Spread the foie gras on toast or crostini to add an extra texture dimension.

Sauternes is also a natural partner for most soft cheeses – its sweetness contrasts perfectly with salty Gorgonzola, for example. For a taste and texture treat, serve chilled with a quality flavoured cheese, a ripe pear and some fresh white bread.

Many desserts are enhanced by a chilled Sauternes. Cooked, chilled pears or peaches served with a raspberry sauce bring out the best in the wine. Most berry dishes also work well with this dessert wine. Soak the berries in the wine with a little sugar a couple of hours before you serve for a perfect match. Very sweet desserts can be too much for a fine Sauternes.

Muscat

Sweet desserts best suit sweet Muscats. Poached pears with cinnamon, for example, balance sweet with spicy, and has a texture that suits the Muscat.

Muscat also works well with the richer desserts, such as chocolate- and ginger-based ones. If serving Muscat, don't accompany a dessert with heavy cream or custard.

Also, avoid serving an excellent Muscat with a heavy, pastry-based dessert, which could coat the mouth and dull the palate.

RICH CHOCOLATE DESSERT

The elegant flavours of chocolate and raspberries are a perfect match for these special dessert wines.

SERVES 4

25 g (1 oz) butter, melted
150 g (6 oz) caster sugar,
  plus extra to dust
125 g (5 oz) dark chocolate
100 g (4 oz) butter
4 eggs
25 g (1 oz) flour, sieved
500 g (1 lb 2 oz) raspberries
icing sugar, to taste
lemon juice, to taste

Preheat the oven to 180˚C (350˚F/gas 4).

Brush four 150 ml (5 fl oz) ramekin dishes with the melted butter and dust with the extra caster sugar until well-coated. Give the dishes a light tap to empty out any excess sugar.

Place the chocolate and butter into a heatproof bowl and place over a bain-marie or a pan of steaming water. Stir the chocolate and butter until melted, then remove from the heat.

Place the eggs and caster sugar into a separate bowl and, using an electric whisk, combine until pale and thick. Gently fold in the flour.

Using a large metal spoon, gently fold the egg mixture into the chocolate mixture, leaving no pale streaks. Pour into the ramekins and bake in the oven for 20–25 minutes, until the desserts have risen, and a skewer when inserted comes out clean.

Blend the raspberries. Add powdered sugar and a little lemon juice to taste, and pass through a fine sieve to produce a smooth sauce.

Remove the ramekins from the oven and place on large serving dishes. Spoon the raspberry sauce around the plate as shown.

Brandy

Brandy is made by distilling wine and then ageing the spirit until it has lost its youthful fieriness. The most celebrated brandies – cognac and armagnac – come from southwest France, but others are produced in almost all the wine regions of the world. In South Africa, Armenia, Georgia, Italy and Spain, brandy production is a major industry.

COGNAC

The raw materials of cognac are the grapes from the Charente region of France, north of Bordeaux – the principal varieties being ugni blanc, folle blanche and colombard. All give a neutral white wine well-suited to distillation. The wine is twice-distilled in copper stills.

The young spirit then has to be mellowed by oak-ageing. The evaporation process and the influence of the wood transform the young brandy into a spirit of remarkable complexity. Chemical evolution gives the wine aromatic complexity and an impression of sweetness and smoothness on the palate. The proportion of new oak employed will also influence the brandy's character. Cognac will continue to develop in barrels for up to about 50 years; thereafter it either becomes over-woody or ceases to evolve. Very old cognacs are important components in top blends, and are usually stored in glass demijohns for future use.

Many cognacs bear a name of geographical origin on the label. The best known is Grande Champagne, the area around the town of Cognac itself. The other regions are Petite Champagne, Borderies, Fins Bois, Bons Bois and Bois Ordinaires. With so many variables affecting the character of cognac, however, the origin of the wine used for distillation may not be so significant.

ARMAGNAC

Armagnac country lies buried in Gascony, well south of Bordeaux. Whereas cognac is dominated by large companies such as Martell and Camus, Armagnac is a complex jigsaw of small estates, many of which bottle and market their own brandies. Moreover, there is a long tradition in Armagnac of vintage brandies, which may not be sold until they are at least ten years old.

CHOOSING GLASSWARE To fully appreciate the complex flavours of a good brandy, use a tulip-shaped glass to capture the aroma, rather than a traditional brandy glass.

AN IDEAL LOCATION *The cognac vineyards cover about 200 000 acres of Charente, France. The climate, soil and coastal situation are ideal for cognac grape-growing.*

Armagnac is distilled in a continuous still, which gives a richer, fruitier spirit. It requires long ageing to express its full potential, and many generic armagnacs are sold too young. Vintage armagnacs are the brandies to go for, and they are often better value than over-packaged luxury cognacs. Vintage dates, however, are less significant than in the case of wine.

OTHER PRODUCERS

Brandies from outside Europe are rarely of high quality, although a few "boutique" producers, such as Germain-Robin in California and Angove's in Australia, have won acclaim.

The brandies of Jerez in southern Spain are highly regarded by the Spaniards, but are not to everyone's taste. Matured in sherry casks and sweetened and darkened with caramel and other additives, they are certainly rich, but lack elegance. Nor are they cheap.

Georgia and Armenia have a long tradition of brandy production, and Winston Churchill was partial to them, but they are not currently available in the West. Cheap brandy is not usually worth buying, except for cooking.

FINE, MARC AND GRAPPA

Thrifty wine growers in France, Italy and elsewhere could never bear to let anything go to waste. Unsatisfactory wine in marginal regions such as Burgundy was distilled to produce a brandy called fine, which is often aged in oak for ten years or more. The lees could also be distilled to give marc, which is also wood-aged for many years. You can find excellent marc in Burgundy, Alsace and the Rhône. The famous Italian grappa is marc in a fancy bottle and often carries a terrifying price tag. But the best grappas can be delicious, with aromas reminiscent of the grape variety from which they are made.

6

In this chapter we look at the three main stages of wine production – in the vineyard, in the winery and in the winery cellar. Local factors such as soil type, climate and the timing of the harvest mean that no two vineyards are the same, which affects the individual style of each wine. This is the reason that wine made from the same grape can taste different around the world. Understanding how and where wine is made is invaluable when identifying wine in a blind tasting, and for appreciating which types of wine you enjoy most.

Louis Jadot, Burgundy, France

The Story of wine

IN THE *Vineyard*

Every winemaker will observe that good wine is made in the vineyard. Soil type, climate and the care lavished on the grapes have a profound effect on the nature and quality of the wine produced – so much so that even neighbouring vineyards can produce very different wines. Getting the vineyard conditions right is the first step in making delicious wine.

VINEYARD DESIGN

Every vineyard has a unique set of natural factors, collectively called its *terroir*. These factors include the soil type, climate, drainage, slope of a hill and altitude – all of which influence which grapes can be grown there, and how well the grapes will grow from year to year. An experienced producer will know how to manage his or her vineyard, to make the most of the natural conditions and to plan for times when conditions may not be favourable.

Natural resources

Location In traditional wine regions such as Burgundy and Tuscany, vineyard sites were chosen generations ago, usually with great skill and foresight. In new wine regions such as Chile or New Zealand, there are certain factors that anyone planting a new vineyard or grape variety will need to consider. These include how much direct sunlight (exposition) the vines will receive, and at what time of day. Incline and drainage are also crucial – vineyards on slopes are usually better drained and less susceptible to spring frosts, but, on the other hand, are prone to erosion. The accessibility of the site also affects the ease and cost of cultivation and harvest.

Climate Grapes need warmth and moisture to fulfil their potential. Climate is probably the most influential factor in wine production. It is the reason why Chardonnay tastes different all over the world, and why vintage dates matter so much in areas with unpredictable weather, such as Europe.

Soil The soil type has a profound influence on the wine. For example, the slate-based soils of the Mosel produce the distinctive flavour of Mosel Riesling, and Chardonnay grows well on limestone soil. Many wine producers argue that grapes do well on less fertile soils where they struggle to grow – an area that might not be successful for other crops might be suitable for grapes.

SOIL *The texture, drainage and type of soil all affect the development of the vines. Stony and rocky soils, in particular, produce many of the world's greatest wines, as they absorb heat and provide good drainage.*

GRAPE KNOW-HOW

The traditional wine-producing regions of Europe have long-established vineyards, and strict legal guidelines about which grapes can be grown where. For new wine regions, there is an element of trial and error when choosing the most appropriate grape variety for an area. A grower can base a decision on areas with similar characteristics, but often the climates are very different. A grower also needs to choose a productive clone (variants of a grape variety) and rootstock (the rooting part of the vine). Some are more productive, or more disease-resistant than others. Unfortunate choices in California led to the destruction of thousands of acres of vineyards by the phylloxera louse in the 1980s and 1990s. Examples of individual varieties that grow well in certain areas include:

- The cabernet sauvignon grape in Bordeaux, France.
- The riesling grape in the Mosel region, Germany.
- The sangiovese grape in Tuscany, Italy.

Training and pruning

Once a vine begins to grow, it is usually trained along wires and pruned to ensure even distribution of bunches, adequate ventilation and exposure to sunlight. In some hot regions including southern France, California and parts of Australia, varieties with low natural vigour such as Gamay, Grenache and Zinfandel are not trained, but allowed to grow into bushes. Growers in Portugal and Italy have trained vines to form a canopy or tunnel, but this is no longer regarded as an efficient means of grape production.

Yield expectation

The amount of fruit each vine produces is affected by all the factors previously mentioned. In addition, different types of grape produce different yields. At Château d'Yquem in Sauternes, the average yield is ½ tonne per acre, which is equivalent to one glass of wine per vine (hence the high price). Areas of Italy and Germany produce yields of over 14 tonnes per acre.

Harvesting the fruit

The best time to harvest will differ according to all the factors previously mentioned. Climatic variations can lead to seasonal irregularities, and the harvest may take place over several weeks if interrupted by rain. Mechanical harvesters allow growers to pick the majority of the harvest at precisely the right time and help to eliminate human error. Many viticulturalists, however, believe that hand-picking is best, and many of the world's top vineyards are on steep slopes that can only be picked by hand.

METHODS OF HARVESTING Mechanisation cuts the time and workforce needed dramatically, but many wineries still prefer the gentler, more selective hand picker. The Villa Maria winery of New Zealand (above) uses both.

ORGANIC WINE

You can now buy wine that is labelled "produced from organically grown grapes", although many organic wines do not carry an organic label. At present, this term is misleading for consumers as regulations vary in both Europe and the USA, and quality varies as with non-organic wines.

Use of fertilizers and pesticides

Until quite recently it was believed that soil could be improved by adding commercial fertilizers and chemicals. It is now recognised that fertilizers can damage the soil, and there is a movement towards totally organic farming and the use of natural compost.

IN THE *Winery*

The basic process for making wine (vinification) has not changed over hundreds of years – grapes are crushed, yeast is added and the mixture is encouraged to ferment, converting the sugar in the grape juice to alcohol. Winemakers work with and adapt this process to make the vast selection of wines that are available to the consumer.

MAKING RED WINE

When grapes reach the winery, they are usually destemmed and crushed to release their juice. In well-established wine regions there will be natural yeasts on the grape skins and within the winery itself, which will initiate fermentation. Elsewhere, it is necessary to add cultivated yeast. Fermentation takes up to ten days.

During this time, any grape skins and pips will ascend to the top of the tank or barrel. Growers can pump the juice over the solid matter, or press the solid matter down with feet or machines to extract as much flavour and colour as possible – red wine gets its colour from the skins rather than the juice itself. Excessive extraction will give the wine harsh tannins, however, and expose it to the risk of oxidation, so the producer has to choose the right moment to stop the process.

The solid matter is removed and pressed separately and may be blended in with the rest of the wine to give it more body. The next step is malolactic fermentation, which converts malic acid in the wine into lactic acid, adding richness and texture. When finished, the wine is moved to tanks or barrels for ageing (see pages 180–1). In some regions, including Burgundy, the malolactic fermentation takes place in the barrel.

Variations

Winegrowers often adapt the basic vinification process. Simple fruity wine for rapid consumption, such as Beaujolais, is made by carbonic maceration, whereby the grapes are not crushed and the vinification occurs inside the grape, protected by a blanket of neutral gas. This makes the wine fresh and fruity. In regions where wine lacks colour, the grapes are macerated first to extract more colour, tannin and flavour from the skins.

REMOVING STEMS Most producers destem grapes to avoid the harsh tannins that are present in unripe stems and to keep as much colour as possible in the grape juice. The grapes are fed into a machine designed to destem and crush them, but the task of removing rotten or unripe grapes and leaves is usually done by hand to ensure that the grape juice is healthy and ripe.

FERMENTATION Many winemakers, especially in Burgundy, still prefer to use traditional wooden casks for the process of fermentation.

MAKING WHITE WINE

The main difference in making white wine is that the grapes are pressed as soon as they get to the winery, which reduces the impact of the grape skin on the resultant grape juice ("free run" juice), and therefore the wine doesn't colour as much. The juice itself has no pigmentation and thus white wine can be made using any colour grapes (red wine gets its colour from contact with the skins during fermentation).

Most white wine is fermented in stainless steel tanks or in large neutral casks and the temperature is closely controlled to prevent loss of aroma. Some wines, notably Burgundy, are fermented in barrels – a policy increasingly adopted for high-quality whites. Malolactic fermentation is optional – some wines, such as Chardonnay, benefit from a reduction in acidity; others gain from the freshness malic acidity can bring. Some white wine is then aged in barrels or tanks. Often wines ageing in small barrels are stirred regularly; this can give the wine more richness.

whole-cluster pressing

Most large wineries destem the grapes before pressing, but at smaller wineries there is a move towards whole-cluster pressing, which gives cleaner juice. Since whole clusters take up more space in the press than destemmed grapes, this is a costly process. After pressing, the juice is left to settle for some hours, so that the lees can fall to the bottom of the tank and be removed.

MAKING SWEET AND FORTIFIED WINE

There are numerous techniques for making sweet wine, but the crucial difference is in the vineyard. Grapes are harvested late, or ripe bunches are dried, to ensure a high concentration of grape sugars. The juice is fermented in the same way as white wine, but because of the high sugar content, it needs more time to ferment. Winemakers must strive to keep a balance between residual sugar, acidity and alcohol to produce a wine that is fresh and complex, as well as sweet. High-alcohol spirit is added to wine to fortify it, which kills the yeasts after fermentation has begun. This gives the wine its high levels of both sweetness and alcohol.

MAKING SPARKLING WINE

With a few exceptions, such as Asti from Italy, sparkling wine is made by provoking a second fermentation in a wine that has already been bottled. The carbon dioxide released by the fermentation is retained in the wine, giving it sparkle.

Champagne is aged in the bottle (*Méthode Champenoise*) for up to six years, giving the wine its richness and its bready aromas. (Inexpensive sparkling wine doesn't have the same extended contact with yeast.) The yeast is then removed and the bottle topped up prior to sale. Because of the high acidity of good Champagne, it benefits from further ageing in the bottle, though it should be drinkable on release.

MODERN FERMENTATION VESSELS Computer-operated, stainless steel vessels make the regulation of temperature during the fermentation process more controlled. They are also much easier to clean than wooden vats.

179

IN THE WINERY

Once a wine has been vinified, it needs to be aged before bottling. This is to refine any tannins, to moderate acidity and develop aromatic complexity. The wine is then stabilized before bottling. High quality wines usually benefit from further ageing after the wine has been released by the producer.

AGEING RED WINE

With the exception of wine intended to be drunk as young as possible, such as Beaujolais Nouveau, red wine needs to be aged prior to bottling. The duration and container used during ageing has a crucial impact on the flavour and quality of the wine that you as a consumer will eventually drink. Red wine develops in structure and complexity if gentle oxidation (exposure to air) is promoted during the ageing process, and the porous nature of oak barrels is conducive to this. Winery cellars usually afford ideal conditions for the wines to age undisturbed, often for several years. Wine aged for only a few months will have fresh flavours, and is far cheaper than wine that has been aged for longer.

AGEING WHITE WINE

Many white wines, including Sauvignon Blanc and Riesling, are bottled while they are fairly young, after a short ageing period in a steel tank or neutral cask. Such wines would usually be bottled in the spring after the vintage, to retain their fruitiness. Other white wines – notably Chardonnay and Rhône varieties, such as Roussanne – are aged for longer, and often in small oak barrels. Barrel-fermentation gives a better flavour than tank-fermentation followed by barrel-ageing.

Winemakers in many parts of the world have adopted the Burgundy practice of lees stirring. After fermentation, a layer of dead yeast cells, called lees, sinks to the base of the barrel. It used to be customary to "rack" (remove solid matter from) the barrels every three months. The lees are now thought beneficial for the wine, giving it a rich texture and more complexity, especially if stirred on occasion. It is now increasingly common to age red wine in the same way.

AGEING IN THE BOTTLE Most wineries age wine in the bottle for months or even years before selling them, as seen at the Louis Jadot winery, Burgundy. This helps the wine to recover from "bottle shock" (a temporary disturbance that can affect the balance of a wine).

Wood barrel ageing

Why in barrels? Long-practised by French wine producers, the original reason for ageing in small oak casks (barriques in Bordeaux, pièces in Burgundy) was to encourage gentle aeration, which allows the wine to develop fully. As a result, the wine may be imbued with oak flavours – similar to vanilla or smoke in red wine and coconut or toast in white wine. Other wood has been used in the past, but oak has proved to be the best for aeration and flavour. A winemaker may choose to age the wines in large casks that will impart no woody flavours to the finished product.

Adding variety A number of factors influence the eventual flavour of the wine – the origin of the wood, the drying process, the porosity of the wood and the amount of charring during the cooperage (barrel-making) process. The younger the barrel, the more pronounced the oak flavour will be.

Paying the price Barrel-ageing is an expensive process, because of the cost of the barrels and the loss of wine volume through evaporation. It is also labour-intensive to monitor hundreds of barrels instead of the same volume of wine ageing in tanks, so oaked wines can be expensive. It has become common practice in New World regions to impart oak flavours by steeping toasted oak staves or chips into wine as it is being aged in a tank – but this procedure is not legal in all areas. Oak chips will not encourage oxidation, but they impart, at minimal cost, the woody oak flavours that many consumers enjoy.

WOOD FLAVOUR Certain substances present in the wood of barrels are absorbed into the wine and consequently have a subtle effect on its characteristics and flavour.

STABILIZING WINE

To ensure the quality of the wine for the consumer, it is usually stabilized prior to bottling. A stable wine will not undergo any more transformations, such as a further fermentation, which is undesirable.

Before bottling, most wines undergo a number of stabilizing treatments. Some white wines are chilled to very cold temperatures so that the tartrate crystals that form naturally in the wine develop early, and can be removed before bottling. In addition, most wines will be fined and filtered (see right). Many winemakers believe these processes are unnecessary, and can affect the quality of the wine.

finishing touches

■ To prevent cloudiness, wine producers introduce a coagulant such as bentonite or egg white, to attract any small particles that remain present in the wine. This process is an effective way of reducing tannin levels in red wine, and making it more drinkable in its youth.
■ Prior to bottling, most wine is filtered to remove any remaining solid matter.
■ If a wine is aged for many years, it may throw a deposit (produce particles). This is not a problem, and is usually a sign of a good, mature wine. You may choose to decant the wine (see pages 128–9) to avoid drinking the particles.

Rosé

Refreshing, fruity wines with luscious flavour, rosés also have an acidic finish. They can be enhanced by a variety of foods and their dryness and tinge of colour can add bite and vibrancy to a meal. Serve with foods that will benefit from their acidity.

WE RECOMMEND	
Canapés	● ● ● ● ●
Salads	● ● ● ● ●
White meat	● ● ● ● ●
Fish	● ● ● ●

Rosé

Whether you choose rosé from France, Portugal or the New World you can be sure that you are serving a wine that will cater to many foods. It is a good choice to serve as an apéritif with canapés or at picnics – occasions where a variety of flavours is the standard. Serve rosé wines well chilled at summer picnics, to soothe the palate and cool you down.

The range of textures and flavours in Greek meze – hummus, taramasalata and tsatziki – can be tied together wonderfully with a lively rosé.

Rosés also are perfect with salads, such as a Niçoise – tuna with hard-boiled eggs, blanched green beans, black olives, anchovies and a balsamic vinegar and olive oil dressing. The mixture of flavours works with the rosé – the wine leaves the palate clean as its acidity is balanced out by the fruit.

Other salads that sit beautifully with this style of wine include prawn and mixed leaf salad with a citrus mayonnaise dressing. Here, also, the blush colour of the wine is matched with the pink prawns. You also could serve a salad of finely diced courgette, carrots, red onions, peppers, lots of parsley and some

chervil, tossed with a walnut and cider vinegar dressing – a crunchy partner for rosé.

The acidity of raw tomatoes can be too much for some wines, but a dry rosé can match the vibrancy and complement it. Serve with bruschetta and raw tomato with olive oil and sugar as a great starter.

But it is not just cold foods that can benefit from rosé's textures and flavors. You can serve a dry, rich rosé with hot soups and fish stews such as bouillabaisse, provided the wine is not too fruity.

As a main course, accompany rosé with chicken breast strips cooked with pasta, green olives, capers and olive oil or chicken with tarragon. Both of these meals incorporate a slightly tart and aromatic ingredient that sits well with a medium-bodied, herby rosé.

There is enough acidity in a rosé to serve it successfully with pork rillettes, a favourite dish of Anjou, where rosés are prolific. Add a side-dish of saffron-flavoured rice and your palate will be further enriched by the play of flavours.

CHICKEN WITH TARRAGON, MUSTARD AND CREAM SAUCE

A light summer chicken dish, delicately flavoured with fresh tarragon, will highlight the freshness of a good young rosé.

SERVES 4

1½ litres (2¾ pints) chicken stock
2 baby spring chickens, each cut into 8 pieces
175 ml (6 fl oz) double cream
1 tsp tarragon leaves chopped finely, stalks removed and reserved
1–2 tsp wholegrain mustard
12 baby carrots, peeled and trimmed
12 baby leeks, peeled and trimmed
12 baby turnips, peeled and trimmed
100 g (3½ oz) butter
salt and pepper, to taste
4 chives, cut into 3 cm (1 in) strips

Bring the chicken stock to the boil in a saucepan, add the chicken pieces and simmer for 10 minutes. Add the cream and tarragon stalks and simmer for a further 10 minutes. Then remove the chicken, cover and leave to rest.

Strain the cooking liquid through a sieve, return to the heat and simmer until reduced by half. Stir in the mustard and remove from the heat.

Cook the carrots, leeks and turnips separately in butter and add just enough water to cover. Season with salt and pepper and boil until just tender. Drain and keep warm.

Return the chicken to the sauce and gently bring to the simmer to reheat. Season with salt and pepper to taste.

Divide the chicken pieces between four plates and spoon the sauce over. Arrange the vegetables over and around the chicken. Garnish with the tarragon leaves and chives sprinkled over the chicken, as shown.

183

Glossary OF TECHNICAL TERMS

Acidity A taste component in wine produced by the existence of tartaric acid in grapes. Wines can have varying degrees of acidity.

Aerate (Also referred to as "breathing".) To expose wine to air for a period of time before drinking to allow its bouquet and flavour to develop to the optimum level.

Appellation Name or official geographic origin of a wine. Part of the system of classification of wines (see below).

Appellation contrôlée (AC) French classification system to register quality wines by region. Stipulates which grape varieties can be grown in a region.

Aromatic compounds Smell and taste components of wine, detectable as "flavour".

Backbone Term to describe structural taste of a wine. The components that give a wine "backbone" are tannin and acidity.

Blend A mixture of wines made from different grape varieties, vineyards, regions or vintages.

Blind tasting Identifying an unknown wine – in terms of grape variety, region, and vintage – by looking at it, smelling it and tasting it.

Blue chip wines The most sought-after wines, recommended for investment.

Body Term used when tasting wine to refer to the sensation of the weight and size of the wine in the mouth.

Bouquet Used to describe the smell of a mature wine. Not to be confused with "aroma", which is used to describe the smell of a young wine.

Cave The French word for an underground cellar, where wine may be stored. The word is also given to a temperature-controlled wine-storage cabinet that can be installed at home to keep wines in optimum conditions.

Chambré French word meaning "room temperature". Often used to describe the ideal temperature for serving red wine, but can be misleading as room temperature is inconsistent.

Château Name used for many wine-producing estates in France. Can be reserved for labelling only the top wines from an estate.

Claret English term for describing red Bordeaux. Formerly used widely in the USA and elsewhere in the New World on the labels of almost any style of red wine.

Classification System for classifying wines according to quality. There are different systems for different winemaking countries.

Comparative tasting Theme used to structure a wine tasting. A comparison of different examples of the same style of wine.

Consignment Method for selling wine. You fix a price on the understanding that you will not receive payment until the broker has successfully sold the wine.

Corked wine Faulty wine that has been tainted by the cork giving the wine unpleasant flavours reminiscent of wet cardboard. This is caused by a mould found in some corks, which can affect the wine. Not to be confused with pieces of cork in the wine, which are harmless.

Crispness A taste sensation often referring to a young wine. Winemakers sometimes choose to age wine in steel vats instead of oak barrels in order to preserve crispness.

Decant To transfer wine from a bottle into a decanter to remove any sediment. Mature red wines and port often require decanting.

Dumb (or closed) Wines that seem to have no smell at all. It can be an indication that a wine is too young or served too cold.

Dry The opposite of a sweet wine.

En primeur (Also known as "futures".) This refers to buying highly sought-after wine before it has been bottled – at least one year before you expect to receive it. This can be the only way to buy very popular, rare wines, and it can be a good investment.

Finish The sensation left in your mouth after you have tasted a wine. A finish can be short or long, depending on the quality and age of a wine. A very long finish can be an indication of a wine that will age well.

Flange-top A bottle with a lip that helps to minimize dripping when pouring.

Flight Theme or system of tasting wines to create a sense of order in a wine tasting.

Fortified Wine that has had grape spirit added to it to prevent further fermentation. Includes Madeira, Marsala, sherry and port.

Futures (see En primeur).

Grand cru French for "great growth". In regions such as Burgundy and Alsace, it refers to a few select appellations or vineyards that produce the best-quality wine. In the St. Emilion district of Bordeaux, the term is used to distinguish the best châteaux.

Hive A ridged shelf for storing wine – made from concrete or similar sturdy material.

Horizontal tasting Theme used to structure a wine tasting. A comparison of different wines of the same vintage.

Jeroboam Bottle size. Bordeaux is six times the normal wine bottle size; Champagne is four times the standard bottle size.

Laying down Storing bottles in a cellar for ageing. Only some wines are suitable for laying down and will mature and improve with age.

Lees Sediment consisting of dead yeast cells, grape stems, pulps and seeds. It falls to the bottom of a vat or barrel after fermentation. The gross lees are filtered out, although in some white wines, the fine lees are retained until bottling to add flavour to the wine.

Length The persistence of flavour and mouthfeel after you swallow a wine. Can be a good indicator of quality.

Magnum Bottle size. Twice the size of a normal bottle. Magnums of Champagne are often given as gifts.

Maturity When a wine has developed so that it is perfectly balanced. Wine matures at different rates according to storage conditions. When a wine is judged "mature" is subjective.

Méthode traditionnelle Traditional method of making sparkling wine, particularly Champagne, approved by the European Union. Sparkling wines made this way have a stream of fine, small bubbles.

Mise en bouteille au château Term found on bottle labels, meaning that the wine has been bottled in the vineyard or château in which it was made.

Négociant French word for wine merchant. A négociant buys grapes and/or wine and either makes the wine from the grapes or matures the wine prior to bottling. The opposite is a grower, who might make wine from his own grapes. Some companies are both.

New World Winemaking countries such as the USA, Australia, South Africa and Chile.

Noble varieties Grape varieties that have been grown for many years to produce some of the finest wines of Europe, and have been successfully planted in the New World. For example, riesling, merlot, pinot noir, syrah, cabernet sauvignon, sauvignon blanc and chardonnay are all noble varieties.

Oaked This refers to a wine that has been aged in oak barrels. White wine can have strong oak flavours.

Oxidation Wine fault resulting from excessive exposure to oxygen. Wine that is spoiled in this way is said to be oxidized.

Palate Refers to the overall impression of a wine in your mouth. It also can refer to the mouth area in general.

Passive cellar A cellar (usually underground) whose conditions – in terms of temperature, humidity and light – are naturally conducive to wine storage. You don't need to do anything to regulate or maintain those conditions.

Phylloxera Vine-attacking louse responsible for destroying grapevines.

Premier cru French for "first growth". In Bordeaux, it refers to the highest rank in certain classification systems, which rate the best châteaux. In Burgundy, it is an appellation for selected vineyards that are one step below Grand cru (see above) in quality.

Provenance The history of a wine in terms of ownership and storage. When buying wine as an investment it is a good idea to ask about provenance, so that you can be sure that the wine is genuine and has been stored correctly.

Reserva/riserva Term used in Italy, Spain and Portugal to describe a premium wine.

Sommelier French for "wine waiter". The sommelier in a restaurant should be able to give you advice on what to choose from the wine list to suit your meal.

Stabilizing A wine is stabilized before bottling and after fermentation is complete in order to ensure that no further fermentation or spoilage takes place in the bottle.

Superiore/supérieur Respectively, Italian and French designations added to an appellation name. The term may denote a better area, or the original area, or may simply imply that the wine has a higher alcohol level.

Table wine A generic term to distinguish wine from fortified wine. European appellation systems, however, use it to refer to all wine that does not qualify as superior quality wine.

Tannin Astringent, mouth-puckering compound that comes from the skin, seeds and stalks of grapes. Mostly present in red wines as these parts of the grape are largely excluded in white and rosé winemaking.

Terroir French word referring to the unique characteristics of a vineyard, such as climate, soil and aspect, which contribute to the characteristics of a wine.

Varietal A wine named after the sole or main grape variety from which it was made.

Vertical tasting Theme used to structure a wine tasting. A comparison of different vintages of the same wine.

Vin de pays French term, applied to French winemaking, meaning "country wine", to describe a wine produced outside of Appellation Contrôlée regulations.

Vinification The process of making wine.

Viticulture The science and practice of grape-growing.

Vintage charts Charts offering ratings of particular wines over a range of vintages. They can be useful to refer to when you are buying wine, but they shouldn't be relied upon.

Vintage declarations In areas such as Champagne where single-vintage wines are not made each year, a declaration is made in exceptional years.

Useful Addresses

Auctioneers

Complete International Wine Auction Calendar
www.wine-auction-gazette.com

Christie's
8 King Street, St. James', London, SW1Y 6QT,
Tel: 020 7839 9060, Fax: 020 7839 1611,
www.christies.com

Sotheby's
34–5 New Bond Street, London, W1A 2AA, Tel:
020 7293 5000, Fax: 020 7293 6255,
www.sothebys.com

Merchants

Berry Bros. & Rudd
3 St James's Street, London, SW1A 1EG, Tel:
020 7396 9600, Fax: 020 7396 9611,
www.bbr.com

Vinopolis
1 Bank End, London, SE1 9BU, Tel: 0870 241
4040, Fax: 020 7940 8323, www.vinopolis.com

Corney & Barrow Ltd.
12 Helmet Row, London EC1V 3TD, Tel: 020
7539 3212, Fax: 020 7608 2234

The River Valley Wine Company
PO Box 1715, Andover, SP11 9XW, England,
Tel: 01264 77209, Fax: 01264 772096,
www.rivervalleywine.com

Direct Wines Limited
New Aquitane House, Exeter Way, Theale,
Reading, RG7 4PL, T 0118 9030903, Fax: 0118
9030130, enquiries@directwines.co.uk

Amis du vin
www.amisduvin.com

Oddbins
www.oddbins.com

Vineyard information

French Wine Tours Direct
The Birches, Chepstow Road, Monmouthshire,
NP15 2EN, UK, Tel: 01291 690231,
www.winetours-france.com

Tanglewood Wine Tours
Tanglewood House, Mayfield Avenue, Surrey,
KT15 3AG, Tel:01932 348720, Fax: 01932
350861, www.tanglewoodwine.com

Winecountry
www.winecountry.com

Arblaster and Clarke Wine Tours
Clarke House, Farnham Road, West Liss, Hants,
GU3 36JK, Tel: 01730 893 344,
www.arblasterandclarke.com

Specialist suppliers

Riedel Crystal
Available from Michael Johnson Ceramics, 81
Kingsdale Road, London, NW6 4JY, Tel: 020
7624 2493, Fax: 020 7625 7639,
www.riedelcrystal.com

Eurocave, The Art of Wine
Unit B7, Connaught Business Centre, Hyde
Estate Road, London, NW9 6JL,
www.artofwine.co.uk

Instant Wine Cellar Company
Tel: 01564 702921, www.instant-wine-
cellar.co.uk

Software
Wine Technologies Inc., (Publishers of Robert
Parker's Wine Advisor and Cellar Management
software), www.winetech.com or
info@winetech.com

Spiral Cellars
Court House, 23, Woodfield Lane, Ashstead,
Surrey KT21 2BQ, Tel: 01372 279166,
Fax 01372 273482, www.spiralcellars.com

Wine Enthusiast's Gift Centre
PO Box 224, Guildford, Surrey, GU2 7GQ, Tel:
01483 458080, Fax: 01483 560695,
www.winegiftcentre.com

Sunday Times Wine Club
www.sundaytimeswineclub.com

Decanter
583 Fulham Road, London, SW6 5UA, Tel: 020 7610 3929, Fax: 020 7381 5282, www.decanter.com

Drinkwine.com
www.drinkwine.com

Food and Wine
www.foodandwine.com

How and Why to Build a Wine Cellar
(3rd Edition), Richard M.Gold

The Wine Academy
www.wineacademy.com

Wine courses
Université du Vin, www.universite-du-vin.com

Wine Educators, www.wineeducators.com

Wine Society of the World
www.winesociety.com

Wine.com
www.wine.com

Mad about Wine
www.madaboutwine.com

Wine Spectator Magazine
www.winespectator.com

Wine and Spirit Education Trust
5 King's House, Queens Street Place, London, EC4R 1QS, Tel: 020 7236 3551, www.wset.co.uk

Le Cordon Bleu wine courses

To learn about the history of wine and the processes of winemaking, plus tasting techniques and tips on buying, storing, serving and matching wine with food with Le Cordon Bleu, contact:

Le Cordon Bleu London
114 Marylebone Lane, London W1U 2HH, England, Tel: 020 7935 3503, Fax: 020 7935 7621, or freephone 0800 980 3503, london@cordonbleu.net

Le Cordon Bleu worldwide

Le Cordon Bleu Australia
163 Days Road, Regency Park, Adelaide, Australia, Tel: 61/8 83 48 46 59, Fax: 61/8 83 48 46 61, degree@cordonbleu.net

Le Cordon Bleu Brazil
Universidade de Brasilia-Asa Norte, Centro de Excelencia em Turismo, CET, Brasilia 70910.900 D.F., Brazil, Tel: 55/61 307 20 10, Fax: 55/61 307 29 43

Le Cordon Bleu New York
404 Airport Executive Park, Nanuet, NY 10954, Tel: (914) 426 7400, (Toll free in the USA and Canada 1 800 437 CHEF (2433)), Fax: (914) 426 0104, lcbinfo@cordonbleu.net, http://www.cordonbleu.net

Le Cordon Bleu Mexico
Universidad Anahuac, Av. Lomas Anahuac s/n, Lomas Anahuac, Mexico, C.P. 52760, Mexico, Tel: 52/5 328 8047, Fax: 52/5 596 1938

Le Cordon Bleu Ottawa
453 Laurier Avenue East, Ottawa, Ontario K1N 6R4, Canada, Tel: 1/613 236 CHEF (2433), Fax: 1/613 236 2460, ottawa@cordonbleu.net

Le Cordon Bleu Paris
8 rue Léon Delhomme, Paris 75015, France, Tel: 33/1 53 68 22 50, Fax: 33/1 48 56 03 96, infoparis@cordonbleu.net

Le Cordon Bleu Peru
Av Nunez de Balboa 530, Miraflores, Lima 18, Peru, Tel: 51/1 242 82 22, Fax: 51/1 242 92 09

Le Cordon Bleu Sydney
250 Blaxland Road, Ryde, Sydney, NSW 2112, Tel: 61/2 94 48 63 07 (Toll free 1/800 06 48 02), Fax: 61/2 98 07 65 41

Le Cordon Bleu Tokyo
Roob 1, 28–13 Saragaku-cho, Shibuya-ku, Daikanyama Tokyo 150, Japan, Tel: 81/3 54 89 01 41 Fax: 81/3 54 89 01 45, tokyoinfo@cordonbleu.net

Index

Acknowledgements

Editorial Assistant Charlotte Beech

Production Karol Davies and Nigel Reed

IT Management Paul Stradling

Picture Researcher Sandra Schneider

Indexer Madeline Weston

Home Economist Lizzie Harris

Le Cordon Bleu team coordination Deepika Sukhwani and Alison Oakervee

Carroll & Brown Publishers would like to thank the following for their help with this project: Anne Lawrance; Gail Jones; Anthia Cumming; Damian Tillson and Nicolle Croft at Berry Bros. & Rudd Wine Merchants; Martin Turner at Michael Johnson Ceramics; Martin Alpren of Eurocave; Rupert Ponsonby at R&R Team Work; Clare Ashdown and Jonathan Crawley at Vinopolis; Alison Vaughan at Direct Wines Ltd.; Simon and Tim at Majestic Wines Ltd.; Stephanne and Simon at Threshers; Shahid Mahmood; Sandra Brooke; Kate Callaghan; and Lesley Grayson.

We would also like to thank the masterchefs from the Le Cordon Bleu Culinary Institutes for their knowledge and expertise:
Paris: Chef Boucheret; Chef Chantefort; Chef Cros; Chef Deguignet; Chef Duchêne (MOF); Chef Pinaud; Chef Terrien. **London:** Chef Barraud; Chef Bidault; Chef Carr; Chef Colyn; Chef Lewis; Chef Males; Chef Paton; Chef Poole-Gleed; Chef Power; Chef Walsh. **Tokyo:** Chef Bourguin; Chef Gros; Chef Guilhaudin; Chef Honda; Chef Kato; Chef Kazuya; Chef Lederf; Chef Oddos; Chef Peugeot; Chef Yamashita. **Sydney:** Chef Boutin; Chef Harris; Chef Salambien. **Adelaide:** Chef Lawes. **Ottawa:** Chef Bernet; Chef Beyer; Chef Chauvet; Chef Côté; Chef Guiet; Chef Petibon. **Mexico:** Chef Martin. **Peru:** Chef Benoit. **Brazil:** Chef Camargo; Chef Geurin. **USA (LCB/CEC):** Chef Bachmann; Chef Palmer; Chef Salvati; Chef Facklam; Chef Bilderback; Chef Parotto; Chef Jones; Chef Hutchins.

Picture credits: 10/11 Champagne Taittinger, Hautvillers, France; 12/13 Vougeot, Burgundy, France; 21 Cognac; 23 Gettyone Stone; 24 (top) Louis Jadot, Burgundy, France; 24 (bottom) Richard McConnell; 26/7 Louis Jadot, Moulin à Vent, Burgundy, France; 28/9 La Agricola, Argentina; 38/9 Berry Bros. & Rudd Wine Merchants; 42 (bottom) Cephas/Mick Rock; 44 Cephas/Mick Rock; 49 (left) Eurocave (model shown Elite range, B2); 49 (right) The Spiral Cellar; 50 (top left) Cephas/Joris Luyten; 51 (bottom left) Cephas/Mick Rock; 52 (right) Paul Wyatt; 54 (bottom) Louis Jadot, Beaune, Burgundy, France; 55 Courtesy of Wine Technologies Inc.; 56 (top) Keith Saunders/Berry Bros. & Rudd Wine Merchants; 56 (bottom) Cephas/Mick Rock; 59 Cephas/Mick Rock; 64 (top) Keith Saunders/Berry Bros. & Rudd Wine Merchants; 65 (bottom) Deutsches Weininstitut/Dieth; 67 (top) Cephas/Diana Mewes; 70 (top) Keith Saunders/Berry Bros. & Rudd Wine Merchants; 72 McCord (www.mccord.uk.com); 73 Nick Veasey/Untitled; 77 Keith Saunders/Berry Bros. & Rudd Wine Merchants; 80 (bottom) Richard McConnell; 84 (top) Château de Sours, Bordeaux, France; 85 Errazuriz, Chile; 86 (top left) Villa Maria, New Zealand; 86 (top right, bottom left) Janet Price; 86 (bottom right) Louis Jadot, Beaune, Burgundy, France; 87 (top left, top right, bottom left) Janet Price; 87 (bottom right) ICEX (Spanish Institute for Foreign Trade); 88 (top left) Champagne Taittinger, France; 88 (top right) Janet Price; 88 (bottom left) Villa Maria, New Zealand; 88 (bottom right) CIVA/Colmar; 89 (top left) CIVA/Colmar; 89 (top right, bottom left, bottom right) Janet Price; 92 (bottom) Keith Saunders/Berry Bros. & Rudd Wine Merchants; 93 (top) Cephas/Ted Stefananski; 94 Cephas/Mick Rock; 95 Wine Magazine; 101 (bottom left) Keith Saunders/Berry Bros. & Rudd Wine Merchants; 102 Keith Saunders/Berry Bros. & Rudd Wine Merchants; 108 Gettyone Stone; 163 Richard McConnell; 167 Cephas/Herbert Lehmann; 169 Blandys; 173 Cognac; 174/5 Louis Jadot, Burgundy, France; 176 (bottom) Villa Maria, New Zealand; 177 (top) Sunday Times Wine Club; 177 (bottom) Villa Maria, New Zealand; 178 (top) Château de Sours, Bordeaux, France; 178 (bottom) Louis Jadot, Burgundy, France; 179 Louis Jadot, Burgundy, France; 180 (top) B.I.V.B./D.R; 180 (bottom) Louis Jadot, Burgundy, France; 181 Villa Maria, New Zealand.